THE MERITS OF SUFFERING

The Merits of Suffering

HEILI LEE

WILLIAM B. EERDMANS PUBLISHING COMPANY
GRAND RAPIDS, MICHIGAN / CAMBRIDGE, U.K.

To all my brothers and sisters in Christ:

LET US ALL SUFFER TO THE GLORY OF GOD

© 1996 Wm. B. Eerdmans Publishing Co.
255 Jefferson Ave. S.E., Grand Rapids, Michigan 49503 /
P.O. Box 163, Cambridge CB3 9PU U.K.

Printed in the United States of America

01 00 99 98 97 96   7 6 5 4 3 2 1

Library of Congress Cataloging-in-Publication Data

Lee, Heili.
The merits of suffering / Heili Lee.
p.   cm.
ISBN 0-8028-4279-8 (paper : alk. paper)
1. Suffering — Religious aspects — Christianity.
2. Suffering — Biblical teaching.   I. Title.
BV4909.L4   1996
248.8′6 — dc21   96-48111
                CIP

Far East Distributor:
Cross Communications Limited
G.P.O. Box 4559, Hong Kong
Tel: (852)-2780-1188
Fax: (852)-2770-6229

Contents

CONTENTS

OUR RESPONSE

OUR PERSEVERANCE

OUR WALK WITH GOD

Foreword

Not many of us as Christians like to think, ponder, or talk much about suffering. However, few of us can escape suffering. And when we do, it far too often causes us to question God.

It is fascinating to me to note how a gifted Asian layman, my beloved friend Heili Lee, addresses the subject of suffering in contrast to the way the average Western Christian thinks of it. In reading this informative, incisive, biblically oriented book, I sense that the author is far closer to the biblical view in his theology and hermeneutics, as an Asian would view the subject, than are most of us in the West.

Heili Lee helps us to realize — and accept — that suffering is a necessary part of God's pruning, a process not to be rejected, but to be accepted as part of God's providential concern, love, and care for his children.

I found myself viewing suffering from a far different vantage point as I read this carefully constructed biblical thesis on this important element in our walk with God.

In no way is this a depressing book. Rather, Heili Lee stresses the eternal goodness and grace of God in each and every circumstance of our lives. Here is a book of careful guidance and direction for the believer who is hurting and suffering, whether physically, mentally, or spiritually. It contains a marvelous message of hope — a heavenly hope.

Unfortunately, much of our evangelical tradition has sought to teach us that once we become Christians, there will be easy answers for all questions. We sing our evangelical choruses and hope that everything falls into place. Because of this, we avoid involvement in complex issues such as suffering, the search for justice, and the search to end the circle of oppression. It would seem to me that the denunciation of injustice, evil, and suffering and the proclamation of God's victory over all forces of death go hand in hand.

Many of the choruses and hymns that we sing repeatedly in our churches represent a spiritualized theology that is seemingly rich in heavenly language, eschatological expressions, and easy promises of well-being. However, these same hymns and choruses are very poor in incarnational commitments, sound reading of God's action in history, and good understanding of God's kingdom promises that we want to see fulfilled in the life of people and communities.

The psalmist continually declares God's faithfulness as the secret that he wants to share with us. He presents to us the one source of help and hope that he knows, as do we: the Lord God himself. As we suffer, we need to know that all are welcome to cry at the feet of Jesus. He himself will cry with us — a cry of pain, a cry of compassion, a cry of understanding — indeed, a cry that calls forth a new morning.

God upholds the cause of the oppressed, gives food to the hungry, sets prisoners free, gives sight to the blind, lifts up those who are bowed down, loves the righteous, watches over the alien, and sustains the fatherless and the widow. When we suffer, he suffers. He has been "touched with the feelings of our infirmities." This is the message that Heili Lee gives us in this significant volume.

TED W. ENGSTROM
President Emeritus
World Vision

Preface

First I must acknowledge God, who graciously let me live to tell the tale — when I should have been buried under rubble. He let the family business fail three times and my businesses too — all due to circumstances beyond our control. I languished for a period, and then on intensive reading of the Scripture, I realized that there is certainly a lot of good in suffering. This is how I started writing *The Merits of Suffering* — during my period of unemployment. I showed the draft to Dr. Ted Engstrom of World Vision; and after reading the script, his reaction was, "Oh dear, what a depressing book! Americans are not used to suffering! You need to tone it down to sell." Months later I came back with a slightly sugarcoated version that he deemed acceptable.

Dr. Engstrom has given me advice on the arrangement of the chapters. He is my mentor, and without him I would have ended up writing the book and shelving it to gather dust. I would like to express my gratitude to him also for writing the foreword and encouraging me to publish it.

Originally I had intended to publish my other manuscript on the relevance and the all-embracing and holistic influence of the Cross in a Christian's life. A Christian must be Cross orientated, Cross driven, and Cross exclusive. This manuscript is a sister to this book. However, it is not ready, simply because I have not meditated enough on it. *The Merits of Suffering* took me about six months to write, but my intermittent afterthoughts and meditation on it took two years. It is when one meditates and reflects and makes refinements that a book achieves its taste, coherence, and relevance of thoughts. This will also give the book a consistent system of logic.

I must convey my deep appreciation for my publisher friend, Mr. Alexander Lee, of Cross Communications Ltd., who helped me to bring this book to the attention of Wm. B. Eerdmans Publishing Company and for Mr. Samuel E. Eerdmans, who agreed to its publication. I write for a pastime, but they encouraged me to publish it.

Finally, I would like to express my appreciation to Elizabeth Yoder for editing my script.

Introduction

Down through the ages humankind has been searching for an answer to these questions: Why is there suffering in this world and how can we overcome it? Following closely behind these is this question: If God is a just and merciful God, why does he allow injustice and suffering in this world? Philosophers have philosophized on it, moralists have expounded on it, religions have embraced it or tried to ignore it, but we still have not seen any solutions to the problem of suffering. Many a well-intended ruler and politician has endeavored to achieve peace and prosperity by trying to root out poverty and vices in an effort to build a utopian empire, but to no avail.

No doubt suffering in this world is too large a subject to be dealt with in this book. So far in human history we have not seen any solution to eliminating suffering. As long as Satan is in this world, there is no peace. And there will be no end to suffering until God puts him in chains at the end of time. However, if you are a Christian who is suffering and languishing in your suffering, then I believe that I have something to share with you from the word of God in the Bible. The teachings in the Bible have been a great comfort and encouragement to me in my suffering. The Bible shows us the way to come into the presence of God, to communicate with him, and to build a closer relationship with him. At the same time, God will enrich our lives and give us the faith to walk with him through thick and thin.

I shall not be dwelling on any rigorous rationale or philosophy of suffering, but instead will seek to show why suffering is the Christian way of life and why, because there is great merit in going through Christian suffering, we need not be afraid of it. Those who have learned the secret of embracing suffering and living with it will find great joy and spiritual satisfaction. In the chapters that follow, we will be dwelling on personal suffering rather than general suffering. What is general suffering? It is the suffering that all people in all ages have to endure, regardless of whether they are non-Christians or Christians. Let me give a few examples before leaving the topic.

1. Suffering Due to War and Political Conflicts

It goes without saying that in every age and wherever humans live there are wars. The devastation of wars and the suffering they cause result in more hatred and the urge for retaliation. Even in times of peace there are still political maneuverings — rigging of ballots, harassing voters, assassination of opposition candidates — all done because of greed for power and benefits. Revolution for a so-called good cause finally ends up with a dictator seizing power. Promises are forgotten and causes lost. Getting drawn into its wake are racial conflicts, sectarian religious conflicts, political partisanship, and mismanagement in government. All these contribute to the suffering of the masses.

2. Suffering Due to Natural Disaster

The planet on which we live is sick. Storms, floods, and droughts are here to stay; and as if that is not enough, Mother Nature throws in more earthquakes and volcano eruptions. We, as intelligent human beings, act inhumanly by poisoning Mother Nature and trying to upset her balance. The more progressive and industrialized we are, the more we pollute our environment. The primitive tribes seem to be much more intelligent as far as taking care of the environment is concerned. The word *pollution* is too mild to describe what we do: it should be called *environmental devastation*. There is an old saying which goes like this: Chickens and curses come home to roost. The new saying should be, What we have polluted the environment with, we will drink and breathe ourselves! We have poisoned our groundwater and the atmosphere from which we derived our drinking water. We taste the insecticides we have sprayed on our crops in our cooking pots. When we clear large forests to build dams, we are contributing to the so-called natural disaster. We call it *natural* because we want to put the blame on Mother Nature. We have even broken the earth's protective canopy of ozone because we want to enjoy air conditioning and spray our hair. We have discovered the use of Freon, which is supposed to serve us, but it turns out to be a destroyer. Regardless of who is the scapegoat, we are certainly the ones who end up swallowing the consequences. The culprit: human greed under the cover of necessity.

3. Suffering Due to Sickness and Old Age

Sickness may come to us during the natural course of life: this we cannot avoid. But there are also sicknesses that are our own fault — we ask for them. For example, there are sexual diseases, diseases arising from unhygienic habits or even from ignorance. There are also congenital diseases and defects that we inherit from our parents. They are not our fault, but the result of the sins of our parents; nevertheless, we inevitably suffer.

Finally, we have old age and its associated infirmities — it is Adam's curse that we all inherit. The time will come when our bodies shall be no different from the dust of the earth, no matter what glory and splendor we were endowed with while we were living.

4. The Suffering of Being

The fact that we live here on this earth as human beings means suffering. God cursed Adam, saying, "In the sweat of thy face shalt thou eat bread, till thou return unto the ground" (Gen. 3:19). We moderns are not much different. Instead of physical labor, we have mental labor that is often more strenuous and tiring. Every day we have to get up early and go to work; we have to worry about feeding mouths, counting pennies, and unending responsibilities.

Even when you are very rich and have much enjoyment, your heart is never satisfied and happy (unless you are a born-again Christian). When you are old, no amount of money is able to buy you good health. You will eventually end up as a senile dummy. Yes, living in the world with our corruptible bodies is misery itself.

5. Suffering Due to Human Injustice

We all live in a world of injustice. When there is injustice, there is suffering. More disturbing is the fact that those who are unjust take advantage of those who are just; the just usually suffer more than those who are unjust. Where there is law, there is still miscarriage of justice. Added to all these are judges — they are still human beings, vulnerable to the arguments of brilliant lawyers or vehement prosecutors; and they also have their idiosyncrasies.

What can we do then to make our life's suffering more meaningful and satisfying or to make the best of it? Apart from the new life in Christ, there will be no eternal meaning whatsoever in living in this world, because the sentence of eternal perdition is on the head of every person in the human race. Accursed is the beginning, meaningless suffering is its course, and death is its goal. Unless we get out of this land of the condemned and enter into God's glorious kingdom, there will be no hope.

In the following sections, therefore, we will dwell on things that are of great meaning: why a Christian must suffer, what good suffering can do to us, and what are the merits of going through Christian suffering. We shall consider why suffering is inevitable, why it is necessary, and how it can be glorious and have eternal significance.

Suffering in God's Creation and Transformation

Chapter 1

Suffering Is God's Natural Order of Things

The Cause

Adam sinned by disobeying God. Through him sin and suffering entered the world. Instead of an endless life in the Garden of Eden, God decreed that all people must die and then stand in judgment before him (Heb. 9:27). Suffering, sickness, and old age will take their toll. We are all under the bondage of corruption and death. The whole universe is under a similar curse: it can fade away. Genesis 3:17 says, "Cursed is the ground for thy sake." All nature was cursed because of Adam's sin, so that from then on there were natural disasters. When nature gives us good water in the wrong place in the wrong amount, there is flooding. When nature does not give water where it should be, there is drought. As children of Adam, we suffer under nature in the same way nature suffers as a result of Adam's sin. We need not ask ourselves why there was such a great famine in Ethiopia or earthquake in Java. Just as human beings get sick because the body does not function properly, so also nature gets sick.

The Ray of Hope

Yes, the whole creation is waiting for God's redemption. God will surely do it when he changes it into the New Heaven and New Earth.

We Christians are waiting for that glorious, incorruptible body that God will give us when we see God again. However, before that time comes, we all have to suffer travail in pain together while we wait for that day to come (Rom. 8:22). Until then, we have to go through life facing the weakness of our body: sickness, aging, and death. We have to face the external harassment laid upon us: political conflicts, natural disasters, and human hostilities, often through no fault of our own. We have to go through life's humdrum routines and responsibilities. Yet we are living under a different flag from the rest of the unbelieving world: we are citizens of God's kingdom and living for Christ. With Christ in us, there is tremendous joy in living here on earth, because there is hope: we can look forward to the glorious day when we see God in heaven.

Whatever we do here on earth for God, whether living or suffering, earns for us credits in heaven. When we do the will of God here on earth, it is as if we do it for God in heaven. It enables us to execute matters here on earth in the same way we execute them in heaven. What we do here continues on in heaven. In fact, we are admonished to store up treasures in heaven while we are here on earth. If God told you that there was a way to make money so you could keep it in heaven, what would you do? You would spend every moment of your life making that heavenly money instead of earthly money. Why? It is because of all the money that you make here on earth, you cannot even bring a measly penny into heaven. This is why the Bible also tells us not to waste time making earthly money, but to spend all our time making heavenly money, because earthly money is perishable, but heavenly money is eternal (Matt. 5:19-20). The Bible also tells us to labor and to suffer for eternal causes. Suffering is the blue chip of heavenly money! It is one of the many things that we can do here on earth to earn credits in heaven.

Preparation for Eternity

By going through this life and its suffering, we prepare ourselves for the life to come. This universal order of suffering and corruption is a necessary prelude to the glorious, incorruptible new creation. This corruptible old creation is the seed for the incorruptible new creation. Because it is the seed, it is indispensable; it must die so that it will grow. Paul refers to this seed as sown in corruption and raised in incorruption (1 Cor. 15:42). The following two verses say, "It is sown in dishonor; it is raised in glory: it is sown in weakness; it is raised in power. It is sown a natural body; it is raised a spiritual body. There is a natural body, and there is a spiritual body." All these are parts of God's order of transformation.

If we realize that life here on earth is the seed of our next life, then all our suffering will suddenly become meaningful and indispensable to us. Everything that happens to us, everything that we go through painfully, and every good deed that is done contribute to that good.

The Way of All People

So when we look at sickness, we can see that evil people get sick and good people also get sick. Those who die of cancer are not necessarily evil, and those who do not die of it are not necessarily good. But we can also see that for Christians, all these become meaningful and purposeful, as can be seen in the chapters that follow. God does not exempt a Christian from the sufferings that belong to his universal order of things, but rather transforms them into eternal good.

All people die, including Christians. But there is a great difference between the deaths of Christians and those of non-Christians. Physically there is no difference — both die and turn into dust — but there is a great difference spiritually after death. The Christian dies to gain eternal life and to live again with a glorious body like that of Christ; but non-Christians, sad to say, die and enter eternal death, the Bible says. Death is the great leveler, but death is also the great divider.

All humans have to toil and work hard to make a living. Even the very rich are not exempt from the worry, concern, perplexities, and harassment of life. The poor are similarly afflicted. Even when we are very spiritual, God does not exempt us from working for our daily bread. Being spiritual does not mean that God will drop bread or money from heaven. The Jews in Christ's time were very much mistaken when they tried to force Christ to be king after they had tasted of the bread and fish from the miracle of the five loaves and two fishes. They were hoping for the Messiah to solve their problem of daily bread so that they would not have to work for it. Paul still

9

had to work for his daily sustenance as tentmaker and to provide for the people who worked for him (Acts 20:34). Paul even stressed that "if any would not work, neither should he eat" (2 Thess. 3:10).

It is God's decree on humanity since the fall of Adam that "In the sweat of thy face shalt thou eat bread, till thou return unto the ground" (Gen. 3:19). When Adam disobeyed God, God also cursed the earth so that it might not bear fruit even if we sow, which is to say there will be fruitless works. Fruitless work shall be the lot of all humanity and for all time. Fruitlessness may be part of our life at times, and we must be prepared for it.

Some people, by God's provision, are able to stay in a monastery to meditate and worship God all their lives, insulated from the outside world and its turmoil. But most of us, who are not so well endowed, have to work hard. God rarely intervenes, in the sense of working miracles, in the routine process of life. He wants every one of us to go through the same order of things. The feeding of the Israelites with manna from heaven occurs only once in history. It is rare for us to find people like Elijah, who was fed by ravens sent by God for three years.

When we work, we meet with frustrations, problems, failure, painful relationships, conflicts, and suffering. These have become part of our lives. Most of us who get married and bear children will encounter the problems of marriage: disagreements, misunderstandings, and friction between spouses and in-laws. Added to this are the problems of bringing up children. We have to endure misfortunes, anguish, and even bereavements. In our old age we will have poor health, sicknesses, and incapacitation; we wither like a flower and fade away.

How We Should Live

Being surrounded by the suffering described above, how should we live? First, we must not be overwhelmed; we must make clear our priorities in the face of seemingly helpless situations. Second, we must surmount all these humdrum obligations of life and occupy a place in the service of God and fellowman. Third, it is God's purpose for all of us to embrace the joy that he has in store for us. To sum up, we must be the overcomers in suffering.

Many of us are driven by the routines and necessities of life. If life is hard and you have to work almost day and night to make ends meet, then you find yourself stepping into the trap of neglect in other things. You get up at the last moment and rush to work without breakfast. Then you come back home late at night, throw yourself on the bed, and fall asleep. Meanwhile the house is like a rubbish dump. As far as you are concerned, you have acted as if no one else existed in the house: you have not spoken to the children for a long time and your spouse's expressions of need and inner feelings have fallen on deaf ears. In short, you are overwhelmed by life.

It is time for each of us to make his or her own "declaration of independence": to free ourselves from the bondage of demand in everyday life and to state our priorities. You can say to yourself, "I will work as hard as I can every day, but I will take at least 15 minutes to talk to my family. I will insist that Sunday is my day of rest, not work; we will worship together, rest our minds, and find bliss and restfulness. I will spend time with my family to show my spouse and my kids that I love them. I will not miss my morning and evening prayer, devotions, and my breakfast too." (I take breakfast as an example, not because I advocate compulsory breakfast, but because it is part of taking care of one's health.) So write down your priorities in life, make resolutions about them, and do them. If a person wills, by God's grace, there is a way.

If we are so busy in our routines of life that we have no time for God and fellowman, something must be very wrong. If it is your job that is the cause, you should consider changing it. If it is the basic requirement of that job and profession to be that way, perhaps you could switch to a less demanding and related profession. You do not need to say that if everyone quits this job like you, then there would be no one to serve humanity! There will always be replacements; and if there are no replacements, then the pay is not right and by supply and demand the employer will have to increase the salary for the job. I say this as a generality and not about the specific ministry God wants you to do.

Who Is in the League?

All the great saints of God suffered. Those who were greatly used of God suffered most.

Noah was the only saint in his generation whom God preserved to propagate humanity. Noah had great faith in God. God had commanded him to build an ark as a preparation for the flood. He suffered. The ark took about a hundred years to build, and it was hard work. He had to hew the trees and drag the wood to the top of the mountain to build the ark. Needless to say, he was jeered at by the unbelieving generation. One can imagine that he was harassed by the hostile generation; they were even worse than those who were in Sodom and Gomorrah. This is why God wanted to destroy the whole generation. It took great patience to endure the "hundred years' mock." Who has the patience of Noah?

Moses suffered forty years as a fugitive in the wilderness because Pharaoh was seeking his life. Then God gave him another forty-year ordeal — affront from the rebellious, faithless, and murmuring Israelites. They were a pain in the neck because they were stiff-necked.

Even David, God's favorite man, was submerged in hardship and suffering all his life. He too was a fugitive — from King Saul and from his son Absalom. David was "perfect before God," as is said in the Scripture, which means that he lived a life that was pleasing to God. Yet he was not exempt from suffering.

Time would fail us to speak of all the prophets, apostles, and saints of God. Paul, the "least of the apostles," wrote most of the epistles in the New Testament. He was the apostle of suffering. Under the inspiration of the Holy Spirit, Paul wrote these epistles, which are of great comfort to those suffering because they were written in the midst of his own great suffering.

Finally, Christ is the captain of our suffering. Without Christ, our suffering would not be perfect. He took our suffering and the penalty of sin upon himself; he suffered and died on the cross. What we have suffered pales in comparison. He, as a great and glorious God, stooped down so low into this sinful world, stretched out his hands to us, and died on the cross for us. This is the great divine demotion and humiliation.

New Order

Even though God has put us in this world of suffering and allowed us to experience all the suffering that the people of the world have gone through, God has an entirely different purpose for us who are his people. He let suffering come to us so that he could teach us to overcome, to excel, and to transcend our suffering. When we run our hundred-meter hurdle, we have to jump over all the hurdles on the way to finish the race. In the same way, God wants us to jump over all the hurdles and obstacles in life to qualify for higher service and to fulfill his purpose for our lives. Non-Christians suffer in the natural order of this world, but Christians suffer in an entirely different order: it is the order of his kingdom. To the world we suffer the way they suffer, but in spiritual reality we are suffering in a different world: it is his kingdom that is to be found in Christ. In order to understand what is said in the succeeding chapters, we have to bear this point in mind. It is the first step in transcending suffering.

To Transcend

When you suffer, have you ever tried to praise and give thanks to God for all the misfortunes and losses? It is not in our human rationale to give thanks for misfortunes; even less so for those who are inclined to superstition, because it amounts to asking for more of it. In any event, many people do not wish to think about suffering and would rather forget about it. Yet giving thanks is exactly what a Christian should do when walking in faith. The Bible teaches us: "In every thing give thanks: for this is the will of God in Christ Jesus concerning you" (1 Thess. 5:18).

Have you ever rejoiced in suffering? It takes great spiritual understanding and faith in God to be able to trust God and rejoice in the midst of suffering, to believe that all these sufferings come to us by the good will of God and that therefore he will see to it that it is to our ultimate good. We even have to go beyond this by accepting the lot given to us by God and being satisfied with it! The apostle Paul has given us his example when he accepted his lot in Philippians 4:11-12: "For I have learned, in whatever state I am, therewith to be content. I know how to be abased, and I know how to abound: everywhere and in all things I am instructed both to be full and to be hungry, both to abound and to suffer need." For many of us, being hungry is far from sufficiency. All of us who live in the Spirit and walk with God to feel happy must transcend all conditions of life. That is to say, we must be in the state of not being affected by anything in life. Life's necessities must not be able to touch or affect us.

Let us not moan for what we do not have, but rejoice with what we already have and thank God for what he has given us. Ask God to open the eyes of our spirits and see the good things he has already given us. Ask God to teach us to count our blessings.

No doubt many Christians would find it difficult to be "raptured from reality." After all, we live in a physical world of reality. Are we to delude ourselves? It is not delusion, but spiritual reality that over-rules our life. It took me 38 years after I became a Christian to see this point! One must see it from a new heart and a new mind. A person must be born again and have a new heart and mind to see spiritual reality. In an unsaved person, worldly and physical reality overrule his spiritual reality, if he has any. In a born-again and fully matured Christian, spiritual reality transcends all physical reality and needs. Therefore we must let the new life we have exert itself by the working of the Spirit. This is why it is so important to reckon our new life in Christ. We who claim to be saved must let the Holy Spirit quicken our new life and let it come to the forefront of our being and dominate every aspect of our life in Christ. This is what Paul means by "work out your own salvation with fear and trembling" (Phil. 2:12). For Christians who have not yet attained this state, the message is not that you are not saved, but just that you have not by your thoughts and actions lived out a Christian life — you must therefore caution yourself; live in humbleness and fear, because you have not even achieved what a normal Christian must do.

The Queen Who Transcended

In 1961, when I was a Senior at the Massachusetts Institute of Technology, the brothers and sisters in our Bible study group decided to pay a visit to Christiana Tsai in Pennsylvania. Christiana was the author of the renowned book, *The Queen of the Dark Chamber*. As a young girl she was infected with a strange disease which left her allergic to light. She had to live in a dark room, completely isolated from the rest of the world. She literally lived in the prison of darkness the rest of her life. Like the apostle Paul, she had prayed to God to take away this thorn in the flesh; but God refrained, and she gladly accepted the plight. Instead of being in despair and sadness, she was full of joy and hope.

As a student in science and engineering, I always ask Why? in all that I encounter, even in metaphysical matters. I went down to find out the reason for her joy and happiness. The fellowship with her that afternoon was the most unforgettable moment of my life. She did not answer my questions, but instead showed me a more excellent way. She said: "When I am suffering, I do not ask God why all this happened to me, but rather I ask God what I can do for him; how I can serve him in this capacity." Her spiritual reality had transcended her physical reality and been transformed into higher service for God. Throughout the years she had ministered to countless sick and weary souls and brought spiritual revival to many.

Those Who Succumb

Just as Christiana transcended the universal order of suffering, others in her generation succumbed to it. Ernest Hemingway had everything a writer could dream of: his novels were very popular and sold very well; he had innumerable followers; he lived opulently. Above all, he was the envy of his contemporaries — he was a Nobel Prize Laureate. Yes, Hemingway had all the fame and honor that a writer could hope for; but amidst his admiring crowd he was miserable because he was lonely. He took up hunting as a diversion, but it did not help. *Time* quoted him as saying, "I live in a vacuum that is as empty as a radio tube when the juice is turned off and there is no battery to plug into." Finally he put an end to his life by shooting himself. His ending was befitting the end of all heroes in Greek tragedy. The ancient Greeks believed that the universe was ruled by a "Time-Spirit" — the Tyrannos. This Tyrannos will make all heroes end in tragedy. This is how our English word *tyrant* is derived. Hemingway conformed to the Greek's Hellenistic ideal: that of a hero having a tragic end.

Everyone who does not have Christ essentially has the same ending spiritually, because they are all in sin and under the rule of the Prince of this World. Without Christ there will be no way out. Humanity will all go the way the Prince of this World dictates. The only way to be delivered from the Prince of this World is to believe in Christ.

Christians have said to God, "Take my life and let it be / consecrated, Lord, to thee." Hemingway did not see his life as being useful to humanity, or even to himself. And he certainly did not think that it would be useful to God, because he was an atheist. He too had taken his life for nothing.

Do you want to transcend this universal order of suffering or just succumb? If you want to transcend, read on!

The Joy of a Christian

Having been translated from darkness into God's kingdom of light, Christians should live in joy and happiness, full of faith and joy. The joy of a Christian comes from the intent and purpose of God that every Christian embrace the fruit of the Holy Spirit, which is love, joy, peace, long-suffering, gentleness, goodness, faith, meekness, and temperance (Gal. 5:22). With the fruit of the Holy Spirit in our lives, we begin to understand the purpose of God in our suffering and the merits that accrue from it and are awakened to joy. In the chapters that follow, we will walk with you through the halls of merits of suffering and learn what God has prepared and intended for us in this life of suffering so that we can reckon with and embrace it.

So let us accept suffering as God's natural order of things. Where there is life, there is being; and where there is being, there is suffering. All nature shares this suffering with us. After we have gone through all our suffering, we who belong to God will see him and be with him in glory.

Chapter 2

Suffering in Conforming
to the Image of Christ

All Creation Cries Out

In the eighth chapter of Romans, the grandest chapter of the whole book, Paul resounded with all creation the suffering and pain that all creatures have to go through in life, regardless of whether they are saved or not. The whole creation has to endure the fate of corruption until the time when the adoption of the sons of God is manifested. That is to say, when the sons of God have been given glorious bodies, then all creation will in turn have its redemption. In preparation for this event, God is already doing his work of preparing Christians in this life. Paul admonishes us to take courage and to live in hope, because all our suffering and infirmities are well taken care of by the Holy Spirit's interceding for us. It is the purpose of God for his saints that all things work together for good to those who love him, according to Romans 8:28.

But, someone will say, "I am an orphan. I am alone and desperate. What good is there for me?" Others will say, "I have served God diligently and earnestly all my life. Now I have lost my job and cannot find another one. My wife and children go hungry because I am dead broke. What good is there for me?" If we look at verses 28 and 29, we see that the good is not worldly good, such as money, gain, and comfort. The good that is referred to is the one ultimate thing: to be conformed to the image of God's Son, Christ Jesus. It is a good that

17

lasts; it goes beyond our grave. This is the greatest and ultimate good that humanity can ever have.

When God first created man, Adam, he created him in his own image. When Adam sinned, the whole human race was plunged into depravity, and the image of God in mankind was lost. Look at what man has done in this sinful world; it is a total degradation of God's image, if it is still in man. However, when we are saved, God wants to restore that image of his to us so that we may be able to live like God again. In this Satan-infested and controlled world, where injustice and unrighteousness abound, we would not be able to change our image by our own efforts. We need the Holy Spirit and God's working of all things that comes to us, including suffering, to achieve the goal of making us more like Christ. This is conforming to the image of Christ. But God is a spirit and has no bodily form for us to conform to; and even Christ, who was incarnated and once lived on earth, did not leave us a photograph or picture of himself. So it is not to his physical image that he wants us to conform. It is his life, his righteousness, his love, and his mind that he wants us to have.

The Way to Conform

Why does God use suffering to make us conform to the image of Christ? To explain this, let us take the example of an actor. First, a good actor is one who is skillful in getting away from how he usually talks and acts and in imitating the person he wants to impersonate. He no longer is himself, so to speak. If he could not forget about himself, he would not be able to do a good job of imitation, because he would still be himself and not acting like somebody he wants to imitate. Second, if he wants to be more convincing and authentic — more like the person he is impersonating — he might go to the place where that person used to live, work, and play and live exactly like him, even getting acquainted with some of his friends.

We could use this analogy to explain, superficially at least, the process of conforming to the image of Christ. The greatest difference is that the illustration above has to do with acting, but we are for real. An inadequate way of putting it is this: to imitate Christ, to try to be like Christ, first we must try to forget our "self," which is not easy. There is that stubbornness, ego, and ingrained habit in us that resists this attempt. The only way to bring it about is suffering. When you suffer, your self breaks down and you lose much of your ego. Second, when you want to be like Christ, you should live the way he lived on earth, especially in his suffering and death. This is why we need suffering — to enable us to know how Christ felt when he suffered and died. To be able to do this, we have to walk after the Spirit and accept the suffering that God has placed us into. It is the Holy Spirit that does the work of changing our lives so that we may conform to the image of Christ. Therefore, all the suffering in a Christian's life serves to mold that Christian to be more and more like Jesus Christ. Nothing else in a Christian's life does it as effectively as suffering.

What is the essence of conforming to the image of Christ? It is to be like Christ and have the being of Christ in us; that is, not I, but Christ. It is knowing Christ and his mind, and experiencing his suffering on the cross. This is a mystical spiritual experience: the human mind cannot comprehend how it comes about. We have to take it by faith and comprehend it by faith. In the things of God we walk by faith, not by intellect.

To understand more, let us go through the experiences of God's saints. For some of you it may be difficult to comprehend; but if you take it by faith and live with the Word of God, you will eventually be able to grasp its meaning. When a boy takes after his father, he talks and thinks like his father. Is there any person on earth who takes after God the way a son takes after his father? Yes, it is David. Acts 13:22 says, "I have found David, the son of Jesse, a man after mine own heart, which shall fulfill all my will." Yes, David took after the heart of God: he thought and felt like God and did everything required by God. This is why he could fulfill the will of God. David went through a lot of suffering in his life, and his suffering made him more and more like God. He is an example of a man who conforms to the image of Christ.

David's Experience

So let us look at the life of David. God loved him and made his covenant with him because Christ in the flesh would come from his descendants. Throughout his life David suffered greatly: in his flight from King Saul; in fighting with his enemies; in family problems; in his beloved son rebelling against him; in his sins with Bathsheba. He was constantly pursued by his enemies. In his suffering, he wrote most of his psalms. When we read in the Psalms about his suffering and feelings, we find certain verses that are prophecies of Christ's suffering. Take for example Psalm 69. David is relating his troubles as if he were in deep water and deep mire. Then in the middle of the chapter, verse 21, he says, "They gave me also gall for my meat, and in my thirst they gave me vinegar to drink." This was fulfilled by Christ in Matthew 27:34, 48. Then in Psalm 22, which is a psalm of desperation and a plea to God to save him, his opening verse is: "My God, my God, why hast thou forsaken me?" The first part of it is what Christ said on the cross in Matthew 27:46. In the second part of verse 16 he says, "they pierce my hands and my feet." This is what happened when Christ was nailed to the cross. We can notice the same relevance in verses 7, 8, and 18 and in Psalm 34:20.

Yes, being a man of God and knowing God's heart, David felt in suffering the same as Christ felt on the cross. His suffering became a prophecy of Christ's suffering! Or we could look at it in another way and say that because God wanted David to prophesy about Christ's suffering, he made David suffer, and even suffer in a certain way, so that his feelings were the same as Christ's feelings on the cross, so that his prophecy would convey not only the truth, but also the original feelings of Christ. It takes a man who conforms to the image, heart, and mind of Christ to feel like Christ.

God has done the same with his prophets like Ezekiel and, the most striking, the minor prophet Hosea. God commanded Hosea to take Gomer, a prostitute, as his wife (it was a divine license from God to go against the propriety of the law to fulfill his purpose). Then came Hosea's heartbreaking experience of seeing his wife being unfaithful. In his sadness and disappointment, he was able to feel exactly what God felt about Israel. He was therefore able to relate to the people how upset God felt about Israel's being unfaithful to God by worshipping other gods. What God felt about unfaithful Israel is what Hosea felt about his unfaithful wife.

Paul's Experience

The apostle Paul's greatest wish all his life was to experience what Christ had gone through when he suffered and died on the cross, so that he might be able to capture that feeling and the throbbing of God's love in his heart — to know and experience God in an intimate way. The third chapter of the Epistle to the Philippians is the inner confession of the great saint of God pouring out the deepest yearning and desire of his heart; it is the experience of the same saint who had the mystical experience of being caught up into the third heaven. In Philippians 3:10-11 we catch a glimpse of Paul's most godly wish: "That I may know him, and the power of his resurrection, and the fellowship of his suffering, being made conformable unto his death: if by any means I might attain unto the resurrection of the death."

Paul had experienced a near death and resurrection in an intimate way. In Acts 14, Paul was in Lystra when the Jews from Antioch and Iconium came and stoned him until they thought he was dead. The way the Jews stoned people to death as a punishment for breaking the law was quite thorough in those days. First they dug a pit and made the convict stand inside it. Then people would start by throwing small stones and pebbles. As the excitement of the people grew, they threw bigger and bigger stones. As the convict became weaker and weaker and finally slumped down, people came near with big rocks and boulders, smashing his body and skull. The convict usually died of external and internal bleeding, especially cerebral hemorrhage, which caused a coma and finally death. Finally he was, naturally, buried in the pit under tons of rock.

Paul was stoned, fell down unconscious, and showed signs of death. The Jews, who had come a long way, were not going to do a sloppy job of killing him; they were going to see his breath stopped and his pupils dilated. Before they left him alone, they went to the extent of dragging him out of the city. Even if Paul was not dead, but only seriously injured, dragging him all the way out of the city would most likely cause death. (Paramedics always stipulate that an injured person not be moved for fear of causing more injury.) Paul's disciples stood around him when he was dumped outside the city, and we would suppose they all prayed. Then Paul suddenly rose up and walked into the city. And the next day he traveled to Derbe! So if Paul was not really dead, then it must have been God's miracle of instant healing. If Paul was dead, then God resurrected him. Whatever the case might be, we could say that Paul had that experience he longed for when he prayed that "I might attain unto the resurrection of the dead."

As we review the life of Paul, we find that he actually craved suffering. He went to Jerusalem despite the prophecy of Agabus by the Holy Spirit. Yes, according to Acts 21:13, Paul was ready to die in Jerusalem. There are very few Christians nowadays who would want to embrace and live a Christian life with a great desire of being in the fellowship of Christ's suffering and with the view of dying for Christ.

Reckon Our Suffering with Christ

If we could make ourselves reckon suffering in the same way as Paul did, then we would feel the power of the Holy Spirit working in us. We would be changed overnight; all of our suffering in this life could be dealt with in a positive and constructive way. Much more than that, it is a great joy, glory, and privilege to enter into the suffering of Christ. The apostle Peter, when he was nailed to a cross, considered himself unworthy of dying like Christ, and requested that he be nailed upside down. Suffering and dying as martyr is the gateway to glory.

When we have identified, entered, and embraced the suffering of Christ, we will be able to experience the love of God in a full way. We will be more and more like him day by day. The preaching of the gospel will be real and effective because we really understand the love of God: the love that Christ had when he suffered and died on the cross for us.

When we have the life of Christ in us and experience every day his fullness and mind, we will be delighted to seek his will in everything we do. When suffering comes, we will overcome it by enduring and going through it. In the process, we need to know how Christ would have reacted and suffered if he were in our place. In reciprocity we also wonder how we would feel if we had died with Christ on the cross. Before we were saved, we looked at Christ as someone who died for our sins on the cross — substitution. After we are saved, we look at ourselves as being crucified with Christ on the cross — identification.

Not only do we identify ourselves with what Christ does, but we also become like him — transformation. Conforming to the image of Christ is transformation, and it will be complete when we see God and receive a glorious and perfect body like Jesus. When we really have the life of Christ in us, there is that inborn nature or born-again desire for suffering with Christ.

Have you ever noticed your little baby girl going to mom's dressing table, taking the lipstick, and smearing it all over her face? taking the powder and padding it all over her? She will even step into her mom's shoes and drag them around the house. She wants to be like mom.

When we are saved and become God's children, we want to be like our heavenly Father: yes, we want to be like Jesus. God promised that he would mold us and make us conform to the image of his beloved son, Jesus Christ. Therefore God wants us to go through suffering so that he can finish his work in us. God is an exacting craftsman: he will not take anything less than perfect worksmanship.

Chapter 3

Suffering in the Annulment of Our Corruptible Nature

Which School of Thought?

Whenever we discuss the old man, the body of sin, sinful nature, corrupt nature, and self, we are faced with a bewildering variety of theological definitions, schools of thought, and opinions that are poles apart. For the case of explaining suffering, we will confine ourselves to the issues of whether our old man is completely dead and nonexistent when we become born-again Christians, or whether our sinful, corrupt nature still exists. From here on, I shall use the term *corruptible nature* rather than *corrupt nature* because it is more precise.

Some theologians, having seen how born-again Christians still experience sin and are not yet delivered from sin into a relatively sinless life, have concluded that the old man still exists when we are baptized into Christ's death. Crucifixion is a slow, lingering death, some of them say, and so the old man still exists. Some theologians, in addition, consider the sinful nature to exist in a Christian. One verse in the New Testament, Ephesians 4:22, seems to support the idea that the old man is not dead: "That ye put off concerning the former conversation the old man, which is corrupt according to the deceitful lusts."

My Stand

My stand is based on Romans 6:3-11, where the Scripture says that we are baptized into his death, buried with him, and raised up from the dead, so we should walk in newness of life. "For if we have been planted together in the likeness of his death, we shall be also in the likeness of his resurrection" (verse 5). My reasoning is this: if Christ died on the cross, he really died; and we who are baptized with him go through the same death. We cannot be half dead. Even if someone doubted Christ's death on the cross, his burial would surely make him dead. Do not forget that the Jewish burial custom involved covering the corpse completely with gluey spice (thicker than the frosting on a cake) and then wrapping it around with many layers of cloth so as to prevent air from getting in, thus preserving the corpse for a long time. It is just like mummifying. So even if one is not completely dead after being taken from the cross, the wrapping and spices will certainly cause suffocation. This is the strongest evidence that Christ was dead — no chance for the swoon theory to stand. There was no chance of survival in a Jewish burial. This is why the Scripture stresses burial. It is a point modern Christians have often overlooked because of their own burial customs.

Then there is the resurrection. If we are not completely dead, our resurrection would only be a recovery. To call it resurrection would be a fraud. How can I entertain the proposal that the old man is still not completely dead or is only half dead? How would it exist together with the new man? A spiritual split identity schizophrenic?

Ephesians 4:22 is not difficult to reconcile. Notice the word *former.* It means the past. Notice also the word *conversation,* which means deeds and behavior. Our old man is already dead, but the old habits and behavior still have a vestige in the flesh; we call it our corruptible nature. It will take Christian discipline and watchfulness to do away with it. As Paul said, bring the body into subjection. Also the verse specifically says, "put off," just like taking off your garment. Does anyone have the power to put off the old man by his or her own efforts? No, it takes Christ on the cross to get rid of it. So we do not really "put off the old man"; we merely "put off concerning the former conversation of the old man"; that is to say, after we are saved, we are to put away our old habits, which are characteristic of the old man. The old man is gone, but the old habits still linger on within our bodies; and we must rid ourselves of these by putting them off.

Notice the phrase "former conversation." Someone will ask, "Without the old man in us, how do we sin?" It is temptation. Christ was sinless, and he met with temptations; and so do we. When we yield to temptation, we sin. When we cherish the corrupt inclination of the flesh, when we meet temptation and yield to it, we sin. Refer to James 1:14-15.

Sinful nature is only a theological concept, an abstraction. The Bible does not even mention it. Even the term *original sin,* which is a deduction of Adam's state passing on to us, is not mentioned. I am of the opinion that our sinful nature is nailed with Christ on the cross: no more sinful nature. Think of our sinful nature as the opposite of our sanctified nature when we become Christians. We have all inherited original sin and its manifestations from Adam; we do not have to be taught to do evil. When we are in Christ, however, we become new creatures. The sinful nature is crucified. The new man, the life of Christ, replaces it.

Corruptible Nature

Corrupt nature is also a theological concept, but I prefer to use another concept for the layman: corruptible nature. Corrupt nature is too close to sinful nature. Corrupt and sinful nature go together hand in hand. We cannot separate or compartmentalize them. Trying to distinguish them is semantic controversy. The term *corruptible* is entirely different from *corrupt* although it sounds similar. We still have a corruptible body when we are saved, because when we die our bodies decay. Associated with our corruptible body is our corruptible nature, which is tied to our corruptible body. I use corruptible nature only as a token word. You could call it by any other appropriate word.

When we become Christians, God gives us a new spirit, which is the new life in Christ. God also gives us a new heart and mind, our soul, which is albeit not perfect; but God renews it day by day until we die, and then it will be perfect. Hence the soul will be redeemed when we die. The body will be redeemed when we see God. Our spirit is saved and redeemed the moment we profess our faith in Christ Jesus, but nothing has changed bodily. Therefore, we may still have bad habits; and we need the Holy Spirit to do his work.

Associated with the body are our physical needs and inclinations (propensities). This is where corruptible nature comes in. For example, when we are hungry, we need to eat. It is not a sin to feel hungry and eat. But often it is very easy to overeat or even become a glutton and to sin. Physically we have our sexual urge and desire, but if it is not channeled properly, in the marriage act, it is sin. So it all depends on the inclination of the flesh and how we control it. Paul often speaks of food for the body and the body for food, and that God will destroy them both. It is a passing desire and will perish easily, so we call it corruptible. If we control our corruptible nature, everything is all right; but if we do not control it and let it run its natural course, we sin. Our soul, which is our feelings, emotions, intellect, memory, and its manifestation, works in the same way as the body. So our corruptible nature is equivalent to Paul's "former conversation of the old man" and is related to the lust of the body and soul.

Living on earth in this body of ours is living "in the flesh"; it is neither good nor bad. When we follow after the Spirit, we are "in the Spirit." When we follow after the lusts of the body, we are "of the flesh." Our physical body is neutral; whether it is good or bad depends on whom we obey. When we follow after the dictates of our corruptible nature we are "of the flesh," and walk after the flesh. Corruptible nature is the lust of the flesh; it is the intrinsic nature and quality of the work of the body. Therefore we should not let this corruptible nature of ours dominate us. Instead we should let the Holy Spirit dominate us so as to do the work of annulling our corruptible nature. This is what Romans 8:13 refers to as "mortify the deeds of the body." God lets suffering come upon us so as to annul our corruptible nature and its dominance.

How we control our corruptible nature depends on our moral traits and makeup. Very often we can see a family of "fatties": mom, son, and daughters. There are, in the family inheritance, traits like gluttony and the inability to control it. There is an old eastern saying: a black tortoise never changes its blood. It means the father who is a playboy will beget a playboy son. We often talk of physical genes in medicine; now we talk of moral genes in the spiritual realm. We do often see moral traits pass on from father to son. The bad moral genes are also part of corruptible nature. We all have bad moral genes of some sort in us, because Adam passed them on to us when he sinned; and we all need to bring them into subjection by the power of the Spirit.

An Analogy

Take as an example an engine. If it is properly tuned, an engine will run well and saves gas. If it is not properly tuned, it will emit black smoke and be a gas hog. Corruptible nature is just like bad tuning. Before we are saved, the engine itself is bad; it breaks down often and is badly in need of overhaul. No amount of tuning will remedy it. After we are saved, we are like a new engine: all we need is to be kept in tune. Even a new engine, if it is not properly tuned, will behave like an old engine. The Holy Spirit is like a good mechanic. He not only overhauls our engine and changes all old parts to new ones, but he also does the tuning so that our engine runs properly. When we walk after the Spirit, he will tune our life. He also puts us in tune with God so that we can please God. On the other hand, if we are the kind of person who walks after the flesh, which is letting our corruptible nature run its course and catering to the lust of the flesh, we will end up not pleasing God; for as Paul says in Romans 8:8, "they that are in the flesh cannot please God."

Bear with me for dwelling so long on the above aspect. It is needed for your understanding of the merits of suffering as annulment of our corruptible nature. I have been studying and pondering over the book of Romans for the past twenty years on various aspects. I do not wish to get into spiritual wrangling; I only want to share with you what has worked for me.

I have arranged the following discourse into two analogies. The first section is for young Christians. The second section is for the more mature Christians. Each section differs from the other slightly in terms of its theological slant.

The First Analogy

We are like servants living in the castle of the Wicked King, serving him and his evil black knights. The servants live in fear, suspicion, and jealousy every day. Then comes the Great Prince of Light and his white knights into the castle to subdue the Wicked King and his evil knights and put them all away into the cellar dungeon in chains. Now the servants and maids can serve their new master, the Prince of Light, in joy, freedom, and delight. When we are born again, Christ comes into our hearts, and so sin and unrighteousness, which was once our master, is put away. We can now serve Christ in joy and righteousness. The Scripture teaches us in Romans 6:19: "For as ye have yielded your members servants to uncleanliness and to iniquity unto iniquity; even so now yield your member servants to righteousness unto holiness." Romans 6:11 also tells us: "Likewise reckon ye also yourself to be dead unto sin, but alive unto God through Jesus Christ our Lord." Reckoning for Christians is just like the Prince of Light telling the servants and maids to say good-bye to the Wicked King and his evil knights for the last time. It will be final; no servants or maids will be allowed to go into the dungeon to visit them again. So the servants can say to the Wicked King in vindication, "You are no longer my master; you may consider me dead as far as I am concerned. From now on I shall be serving the Prince of Light." Reckoning is our conscious final break with sin. As far as status is concerned, the moment we are born again, we have already broken with sin, in the same way as the servants have their clean break with the Wicked King the moment the Prince of Light subdues the Wicked King.

Unfortunately, there are some servants who, because of their past friendship with the evil black knights or the Wicked King, still cherish their friendship. They go into the dungeon, secretly visiting them and offering them services. When the Prince of Light knows about it, he will have them whipped. Very often we Christians are very much the same way. We go back to our old buddy of sin and end up getting chastised by God. When we become Christians, do we stop sinning immediately? Not necessarily; but there are great improvements in that we no longer live in sin continually. We do still sin now and then, even quite persistently in certain areas and habits that are our weaknesses. How often have we found ourselves telling a lie, hating somebody, being greedy, loving money, being vain and even sensuous when we knew quite well that we should not? This is why suffering comes into our lives. Yes, God whips us just as the Prince of Light whips his servants who revisit the dungeon. One of the purposes of suffering is to annul our corruptible nature and lust of the flesh, to put it under subjection. (For those of you who believe the old man still lingers on after you become a Christian, suffering is meant to annul the working of our old man.)

In this analogy, temptation is just like the evil knights calling to the servants, "Remember when we were buddies? The Prince of Light is away, so come down and play with us. We promise not to get you into trouble, come down!" If you go down to play with them for a minute, you will end up playing for another minute, and another minute . . . another . . . !

A wise and good servant is one who, after the Prince of Light has put away the evil mob into the dungeon, would clean up all the souvenirs and instruments of vice and throw them away. When we become Christians, we would throw away all the pornographic magazines, tapes, erotic rap records, and other instruments of lust and bad habits; we would put away even the reminders of past sins. One great help is to keep away from temptation. Have you often felt that other people were getting away with a lot of bad deeds — getting away with murder, so to speak — and you would get caught in the slightest offense? You may even ask God why he is unfair because he does not protect us from being caught or give us better luck? No, it is God's goodness that he lets us get caught; it is his chastisement. He lets us suffer so that we dread sin like a child who gets burned and then dreads the fire, so that we can learn righteousness and approach a sin-free life as much as possible. We will never attain sinlessness until we see God, but our goal is to run towards perfection. "Be ye therefore perfect, even as your Father which is in heaven is perfect" (Matt. 5:48).

The easy money that makes you filthy rich won't buy you holiness. Getting away with murder is not good luck; it is Satan's sweet way of leading people into perdition. Beware of Satan — he knows how to make an offer you will find difficult to refuse!

The Second Analogy

For the mature Christian, the second analogy starts out like the first, but it goes a step further:

When the Prince of Light subdued the Wicked King and his evil black knights, he put them away into the cellar dungeon. He made the servants say good-bye to them and then left the castle, taking the servants along with him and sailing off to a far-away land where his own castle is. So the servants cannot come back to visit those that are in the dungeon. This is analogous to Christians who reckon themselves dead to sin. Notice the real meaning of *dead*. The only way that we can leave this world is to die. When we are dead in one realm, we no longer exist in that realm; we end up in another realm.

Before we were saved, we were in the realm of sin. After we are saved, we end up in the realm of righteousness and of his kingdom; therefore, we cannot visit the realm of sin again. It takes faith to reckon that we are no longer under sin, because our daily living often seems to belie that state. It is just like believing that we have eternal life when actually we are in a state of death. We must live beyond our human sight and perception and by faith develop into the man walking after the Spirit. A mature Christian must be living under the realization of a new life in God and in a realm that is not of sin, but of righteousness. He or she must live under the positive attitude of having been delivered from the bondage of sin through the Cross, and believe that by the power of the Holy Spirit and the blood of Christ he or she is sanctified and can therefore overcome sin and temptation. This person could look at the conflict of the two laws in Romans 7 and say, "Thanks to God I am delivered from this conflict; sometimes/rarely I may have this conflict, but it is the exception rather than the rule."

Where do temptation and sinning come in then? The servant who is unable to communicate with the black knights in the dungeon can still have wrongdoings and mischief. Whereas in the old castle, before the Prince's conquest, the servant's wrongdoings were ordered by the black knights, now, under the Prince of Light, his wrongdoings originate from himself. This is because he still has his bad habits and the memories that linger in his mind. It is his trace of corruptible nature residing with the flesh. Every time he bows to the cravings of the flesh, he yields to temptation. The Prince will whip him still — it is just like God letting suffering come to us to teach us a lesson.

In both analogies the old man is equivalent to the servant serving the wicked king and his evil black knights, and the new man is equivalent to the servant serving the Prince of Light. I have used function to define form so that you can understand. Actually, the old man and the new man are better understood not as a person or form, but as our propensity and identity personified. We know it exists because the Bible has said it, and we have observed its functional manifestation.

If we take a tripartite view of ourselves as spirit, body, and soul, what part of it constitutes the old man or new man? It is the propensity

31

of our spirit, body, and soul to go in a certain direction and its manifestation that determines whether we are in the old man or new man mode. Paul personified these functional manifestations so that we can understand them more easily. The same thing applies to his term "body of sin." We will never understand fully the meaning of these terms because so little of them is mentioned in the Bible, but we will understand them when we see God in the glorious body that he gives us.

Before we are saved, our spirits are dead and cannot communicate with God because they are separated from God by sin. Our souls and bodies follow the dictates and lusts of our corruptible natures and also Satan; this is our old man mode. When we are saved, our spirits come to life again. The Holy Spirit has raised our dead spirit, which has been crucified with Christ. This new living spirit has the life of Christ; our soul and body move according to the guidance of the Holy Spirit. This is the new man mode.

To be more exact, this is really the life of Christ. To say it in a less daring way, it is the life of Christ in us. Such a statement is based on what the apostle Paul said in Galatians 2:20: "I am crucified with Christ: nevertheless I live; *Yet not I,* but Christ liveth in me. . . ." The phrase *Yet not I* means that after the crucifixion there is a complete change of identity. My "I" disappears from the scene. Taking its place is Christ. Paul then makes it easier for the reader to understand by saying that it is Christ who lives in me.

Please do not for a moment think that it is still "I" that is living and that Christ is the guest in me! Many of the Christian writers meant well by saying that Christ is the guest at every meal and the silent listener in every conversation. Yet when we read the book of Romans, we invariably find that Christians must live under the dictates of God; that is, we must strictly follow the dictates of the Holy Spirit by walking after the Spirit. This is the only way to deliverance from sin, according to Romans 8. The Christian's life is a mandatory life; we live under the mandates of God. This is why the Lord's prayer says "Thy will be done."

Whereas before we are saved there is no Spirit to lead us, after we are saved our body and soul can follow the leading of the Holy Spirit — all the while our spirit is the message bearer of the Holy Spirit, telling the body and soul what we should do. After all, the part that communicates with God is our spirit. Having understood all this, we now should think of ourselves as one person and take a holistic view of ourselves instead of putting blame on any part of ourselves such as body or soul. We are ultimately responsible for what we do as persons.

Having said all the above, we should also realize that after we are saved our bodies and souls can still choose to follow our residual corruptible nature, sin, and Satan. For this reason God lets suffering come upon us to teach us to walk after the Spirit.

Christians who are not convinced that their regenerated lives are the life of Christ in them and not their own will live defeated lives. These Christians have been influenced by the disappointing behavior of their body and soul and afraid of believing that it is possible for the life of Christ to be in them.

All of this may be difficult for the average layperson to understand. But as you live on and mature spiritually, you will begin to grasp some of the meaning of the above discussion. For now, let us remind ourselves that the gospel is the gospel of a new life in Christ — new living, not new intellect! The mystery of God is better understood by babies than by sophisticated grownups.

Thoughts for Intellectuals

Let us take another analogy. Our spirit, body, and soul are analogous to the computer hardware, and the old man or new man (new life) to the software. How the computer runs depends on the software. Corruptible nature is the "bugs" in the software, or even the virus. Before we are saved, we are just like a defective old computer running on software that is full of bugs. Even when we are saved, we are like a new powerful computer loaded with new software, albeit still with a little bug. The bug is of the type that does not seriously affect the program, but just now and then throws some unintelligible words on the screen or freezes up the program so that one has to reboot the computer again. It will take time to identify and root out the bugs in the program. Corruptible nature is like that described in the Song of Solomon, where "the little foxes . . . spoil the vine" (Song 2:15).

In order to apply all these to our lives, we need to go through the spiritual identification of our old man being crucified with Christ: "Knowing this, that our old man is crucified with him, that the body of sin might be destroyed, that henceforth we should not serve sin" (Rom. 6:6). Every Christian and theologian is talking about it, but

33

what is it in real life? Accept that the whole thing happened to me by faith. It is just like believing that Christ suffered and died on the cross and rose again, so I believe that I too have been crucified with Christ at the same time. Living every day with the daily reckoning of being crucified with Christ will enable us to overcome the lust of the flesh trying to motivate all aspects of our life. More importantly, it annuls the self that has been trying to gain control and exert itself. In the same way that we believe Christ was crucified on the cross and that this brings us the righteousness which is by faith, reckoning that we are crucified with Christ brings us into righteous and sanctified living.

In simple terms, God has provided us with a way to annul the working of our corruptible nature by identifying ourselves with the crucifixion of Christ. And when we suffer, we identify our suffering with the suffering of Christ. From here on the power of the Holy Spirit takes over. We do not need to rely on the effort of the flesh to improve ourselves, but by faith live on and claim the power of the Holy Spirit in leading us into a victorious life.

Suffering in God's Family

Chapter 4

Suffering as Children of God

Whose Children Are We?

We are living with the children of Satan. We are different from Satan's children, so Satan and his children will naturally hate and persecute us. God wants us to be different from the rest of the world and to walk as children of light. To this end, God needs to instruct us and even chastise us when we do wrong so that we may be brought up as children of God.

Very often when I am ostracized and discriminated against, it is because I am a Christian. I always remind myself that I do not belong to this world, and therefore the world hates me. Indeed, it is really Christ that the world hated in the first place. However, everything that is in the world, strictly speaking, belongs to God; and he has full jurisdiction over it. But Satan is a usurper, and God chooses to let it be for the moment, so that his children can learn to overcome the world through faith. God wants to teach us how to fight spiritual battles. This world is our "boot camp," where like new military recruits we go through hard training.

Being Children of God

"My son, despise not the chastening of the Lord; neither be weary of his corrections: for whom the Lord loveth he correcteth: even as a father the son in whom he delighteth" (Prov. 3:11-12). Being children of God would also mean that we have to go through chastisement, in the same way that children are disciplined by their father. Remember your childhood days when you were full of mischief and being a menace? Remember how you were scolded and spanked? As far as God is concerned, we are just as naughty spiritually, and in need of correction. When we become Christians, we are like slaves of sin becoming princes of God — the children of God. What a change! It is just like a pauper becoming a prince; there is so much to be learned. Teaching us to know the things of his kingdom is just like bringing aborigines from the wild and teaching them how to speak, read, write, and live like civilized people: there is a tremendous amount of adjustment. We are also like babies, little children, in the matter of righteousness. We were evil and sinful by nature and now we are entering into a life of righteousness and holiness. How shall we be sufficient for this new life? The Scripture tells us that God, when he accepts us as his children, also chastises us so that we may learn to be righteous and attain unto holiness (Heb. 12:10-11). It is just like bringing up a child at home so that he or she may grow up to be a person of good character and principle. It takes a lot of work to bring up a child; therefore, if the child is not your own, then you would not even bother to teach and discipline him or her because it takes too much effort. If we are not God's children, then God too would not chastise us. He would give us up to the lust of our flesh the way God gave up those who did not wish to acknowledge God, as mentioned in the first chapter of Romans.

We Children

Unfortunately, most of the modern-day children have never experienced physical discipline from their parents. Even if there was such discipline, it stopped short at an early age. Many folks of our older generation have experienced being spanked, caned, slapped, and ordered to go to bed without supper. We were brought up the Victorian way. None of us ever doubted that it was the right way. We enjoyed telling — without any resentment at all — anecdotes of how naughty we were and how our parents gave us a good spanking. Not only does being physically disciplined by our parents not create any resentment or psychological scar, but it even creates a firmer bond between children and parents. It gives the child a sense of belonging. If you were to ask me what I remember about my father and mother most, I would say that it is not so much that they fed and clothed me as their earnestness in teaching me right and wrong. Never was the cane spared, and never could I get away with wrongdoing. They poured out their love and expectations of what they wanted me to be — a righteous and a great man.

The Two Sides of My Mother

I can still remember my childhood days when I kept getting sick all the time. I would get a splitting headache in the night, and my head would roar like a roller coaster. I saw markings on the walls coming alive and becoming moving cartoons. They all jeered at me, then disappeared, giving me a sight of relief; but suddenly they were all back, doing their tantalizing acts again. As the fever got higher, I felt as if I was put into a drying tumbler. The tumbler was like a long tunnel: I was rolled from one end of the tunnel to the other and back again. I cried to my mother, and she was by my bedside holding my hands. It was such a relief. Her words of comfort soothed me. Very often she was by my bedside day and night. Even now I still cannot figure out how she managed her sleep. I cannot forget my mother's kindness and love. In all my childhood days she made me feel that I could never live without her. Even when I had a problem she always had the answer.

Yet this mother could give me a good spanking when I did wrong and got into mischief. In my young heart I could not understand how my mother, who could be so sweet to a sick child, could be so severe and martial-like and be a roaring lioness to me when I did wrong. It seemed that she had two sides to her character.

When I grew up and had children of my own, I suddenly realized what all these meant. To my kids I seemed to have two sides to my character. But I know that when I love my children I must take care of them physically as well as morally. Now I realize that when I was sick my mother took care of me physically; and when I was sick morally, she then took care of me morally by spanking me.

In very much the same way, God takes care of us physically by giving us rain, sunshine, and harvest as well as his protection in life.

He takes care of us morally and spiritually by chastising us so that we may be righteous and holy.

Spoiled Kids

But there is another school of thought — some schools of modern child psychology advocate that beating a child will leave scars in their lives that will turn into repressed sentiment. Perhaps too, some modern parents do not know how to bring up their children; and some even go overboard into child abuse. The society at large does not even permit the physical discipline of our children for fear of mistreating them. As a result, many modern children are not able to tell the difference between being spanked out of love and being abused out of hatred by their parents. So it turns out that the tendency is for parents to over-pamper their child: they are given what they want. Parents are afraid of putting pressure on them; consequently, they grow up spoiled and undisciplined. Then they go into society and find themselves misfits. They are not able to get along with their colleagues. When their bosses give them a piece of their mind, they simply fall apart. The tragedy is that they mill around from job to job looking for easy work and heavenly treatment, but of course find none. They are the misfits of society. God forbid that we Christians should be turned into "spoiled Christians." God will never let us get away easily. You may bring up your child the way you like. As for God, he is going to discipline us the old-fashioned way — with a rod, as the Bible puts it, regardless of whether we like it or not.

God's Way with His Children

The book of Hebrews tells us what God wants to do with us as his children: "For whom the Lord loveth he chasteneth, and scourgeth every son whom he receiveth. If ye endure chastening, God dealeth with you as with sons; for what son is he whom he chasteneth not?" (12:6-7). This is how God deals with every one of us when we become Christians. We should be prepared to take lessons from God. Since God, unlike our parents, never makes any mistakes, we can rest assured that we are in good hands, whatever suffering and calamity we encounter. Whatever comes to you, take it in faith and give thanks to God. Asking God why is equivalent to doubting God's judgment and capacity. Even wanting to know why out of curiosity often undermines the perfection of faith in walking with God.

Whose Fault?

How much assurance does one have when one is chastised of God that the matter comes from God? What if one does wrong and suffers because of sin, can one say that it is a chastisement from God or that it is a consequence of sin and it serves one right? Let us take a real-life example. A seminary graduate was called of God to become a missionary in the remote jungles of Africa. Trying to avoid hardship, he backed away and became the pastor of a church in the city. He got married and had a handsome and intelligent boy. One day the little boy fell down from a high chair, broke his neck, and died. The pastor was full of remorse for the rest of his life, so the story goes. Many of his Christian friends are of the opinion that if he had heeded God's call, then he would not have lost his son. I am of the opinion that this is not necessarily the case. It is just like telling Job, "You lost all your sons because somewhere along the line you did something wrong."

If the pastor had heeded God's call to go to Africa, he may still have lost his son, or he may not have; we do not know the purposes of God. But the main point is that if he had heeded God's call, then come what may, he would not be blaming himself because he had done God's will. He would have a clear, clean conscience to face suffering, misfortunes, and calamities. But if he does not heed God's call, then whatever mishaps come in life, he would find himself examining his conscience all the time to determine whether it is his fault or entirely from God.

If we obey God and do his will, then whatever disaster comes to us, we still have peace and a clear conscience because it comes from God. Whereas if we do not walk according to the will of God, then whatever calamity comes to us, we will have no peace. We will be trying hard to determine whether it is the result of our wrongdoing or whether God had to do it regardless.

41

The Lordship of Christ

When we have Christ as Lord of our life, taking full control of everything, we will have great peace in our hearts because he is fully responsible for whatever happens. Our future and destiny are in good hands because the all-wise God never makes any mistake.

If we do not take Christ as our Lord, then there is total irony. Here we are calling ourselves children of God, and yet we do not want God the Father to have any jurisdiction over us. Not having Christ as Lord and God is equivalent to not calling God our Father. What it amounts to is that we go to God and want God to treat us like his children, to provide for us like a father, and yet we tell God that we do not wish to obey him nor consider him our father!

Yet there are some theologians who advocate: "Just say you believe in Christ, and your salvation is secure; not taking Christ as Lord does not affect your salvation." What they are trying to do is to separate the salvation of God and the lordship of God into two packages, so that we lost sons of Adam can still have the choice of taking salvation without God's lordship. Christ teaches that we can only serve one master in life: God or mammon (money); this is the way God looks at it. Don't try to deceive yourself that you can serve money and God at the same time. When God is not our master and lord, then money becomes our master; and God will not have anything to do with us once we serve mammon and reject him as our master.

It is by the grace of God that many of us who once did not take Christ as Lord eventually take him to be Lord. Those who take Christ as Savior only and not as Lord must be prepared to examine whether they are really saved in the first place. We have seen too many so-called believers falling away from God because they do not take Christ as Lord. I believe in the assurance of eternal salvation when Christ is my Lord. He cannot do the work of salvation in me unless I let him be my Lord. God will not force us to be saved if we do not accept him and receive him as Lord. "As many as received him, to them he gave power to be the sons of God" (John 1:10). The Scripture specifically mentions "receive him." What is "him"? He is God and Lord. The better way is to accept him as Lord and then as Savior, according to Romans 10:9. Technically, in the spiritual sense, when you accept Christ as Lord, he will do the work of salvation in you. Many a

42

Christians has struggled for years before yielding completely to Christ and taking him as Lord. By the grace of God he suffers their folly and keeps them from falling away in the meantime. Some who take too much advantage of God fall away. Others are more blessed; they take him instantly.

When Christ is our Lord and we suffer, Christ suffers with us also because Christ said, "The reproaches of them that reproached thee fell upon me" (Ps. 69:9). It is a comfort to know that when we suffer, Christ is with us; and we know that it is for a purpose that we may not know now. But we are sure that for us all things work for good because we love God, and because we are called according to his purpose (Rom. 8:28). And God has not ceased reminding us that it is for his good will and purpose. Therefore, when Christ suffers with us, he will never desert us; and we shall never fall away.

God Cares for His People

God cares for his suffering people. He will do his work of deliverance when the right time comes. The history of Israel has always been filled with episodes of God's deliverance of his people.

Let us look at the saddest and the most desperate moment in Israel's history. The whole race was facing extermination under the rule of the Pharaoh who did not know of Joseph's great deeds. God had chosen and raised up Moses for the task. But before he was fit for being an instrument of God's deliverance, there was something God wanted him to see as God sees it. Moses had seen the people of Israel suffer. It was as if he had seen the suffering Messiah who bore the reproach of his people (Heb. 11:25-26). Therefore Moses would rather suffer along with the children of Israel and to bear the reproach of Christ than to enjoy the pleasures of sin in the court of the Pharaoh. It seems as if Moses had seen the vision of the suffering Christ and therefore dared to move against the interest of all his worldly advantages and to sacrifice all that is precious in man's sight.

God tried his heart when he was a shepherd in the desert for forty years. God molded his character and made him the most humble man there is: yes, God wanted to refine the vessel he intended to use. Moses had gone from the pleasures of the children of men to the suffering of the children of God and finally suffered in the spirit of

Christ. Therefore God appeared to him in the burning bush. The bush was on fire and yet not consumed. The children of Israel suffered under fiery trials and yet were not consumed. It was God who kept his own people and made them persevere. Christ suffered the fiery trials of death and yet was not consumed because he rose triumphantly from death.

In the burning bush God declared that he was the "I am." Christ is the revelation of that "I am" in the flesh. From the burning bush, Moses had received a mission from God — to lead the children of Israel out of the bondage of Egypt. The vision of Christ caring for his suffering people and the divine compassion of God for his suffering children so captivated Moses that he decided to move in faith as a response to God's calling. It was this vision of mission that kept Moses persevering for forty years in the desert, leading the people of Israel into the promised land. He persevered in the midst of a murmuring, bickering, and rebellious people, even though from the very start, at the waters of Meribah, Moses was told by God that he would not reach the promised land (Num. 20:13). Yet he did not give up during all those forty years. A lesser and more pragmatic person would have given up long ago.

If these people were not the children of Israel, then there would be no vision to Moses. If Moses had not seen the vision, then the children of Israel would have perished in Egypt within one generation.

God cares for his own children, and he wants his children to accept his chastisement.

Yes, it is a blessing to suffer as children of God.

Chapter 5

Suffering in Fellowship

Our Glorious Partnership

The fellowship of suffering is a God-given gift. The fellowship of suffering of the body of Christ and the fellowship of Christ's suffering together are the great, glorious partnership we have with Christ (Phil. 3:10; 1 Peter 4:13; 1 Cor. 12:26).

Suffering Together

To understand this God-given suffering, we need to understand human suffering, especially that of a family. The most obvious sharing of suffering in a family is that which is shared between husband and wife. The husband's problems and suffering usually become those of the wife and vice versa. The more they are able to bear each other's suffering, the more deeply they understand each other. Suffering is always compatible with love. The more you love a person, the more you care for him or her; and when he or she suffers, the more you suffer with him or her. By the same token, when your children suffer, you suffer also. Very often a mother suffers for her children more than she suffers for herself and worries for her children more than she worries for herself. On the other hand, when you hate a person, you don't care what that person goes through; you would never want to share that person's suffering and burden.

For the members of the body of Christ to suffer together and share with each other their suffering, there must be that love and tie that binds the members together as one body. There must be that same goal and sense of mission in God: the same hope, vision, and unity of mind. This is the human aspect.

Then there is that supernatural aspect — God's allowing us to suffer and to feel the suffering of others even though we are far from each other. The Old Testament prophets have often keenly felt the suffering of the people of Israel and interceded for them before God. The apostle Paul took the care and concern of the churches of Asia Minor upon himself — he felt their sorrow and joy (2 Cor. 11:28, Phil. 1:4-8).

The Human and Divine Partnership

When God first created humankind, he put in it the nature of mutual dependence and the propensity of fellowship. When God first created Adam, he looked at him and immediately said, "It is not good that the man should be alone; I will make him an help meet for him" (Gen. 2:18). This is why Eve was created. Yes, man needs woman, and woman needs man. The relationship must be so close and intimate that it can function as one entity. Marriage, that mystical union of man and woman, is a fulfillment of that entity. But it does not stop here. There is that even more mystical union of God and man: Christ as the Bridegroom and the church as the bride. Above all, there is that ultimate mystery of the Trinity — the union of the Father, the Son, and the Holy Ghost as One God.

When a man and woman are united, they share with each other joy and happiness as well as sorrow and suffering. Similarly, when Christ is the Bridegroom or head of the body, there is the sharing of joy and sorrow, happiness and suffering. How does it work? When Christ suffered on the cross, we also suffer with him; we believers are identified with his suffering. We experience in a vicarious way the suffering of Christ on the cross. The reader can refer to Chapter 2 above on "Suffering in Conforming to the Image of Christ." When we suffer, Christ also suffers. This can be seen in the life of the apostle Paul (Saul). He was persecuting the church; and one day on his way to Damascus to persecute more Christians, God blinded him with a light from heaven and said, "Saul, Saul, why persecutest thou me?"

(Acts 9:4). When Saul was persecuting the church, he did not realize that it was actually Christ that he was persecuting. So when the church suffers, Christ suffers.

Similar to the fellowship of husband and wife is that between parents and their children. Among all the creatures of God, we human beings need the longest period of parental care. The lower animals need a much shorter period of care. God has made that period to be long so that parents can take time to bring up their child, to share the teachings of God in the Scriptures, how he or she should live, how he or she should love God and neighbor. They can also share their spiritual and life's experience with their child. When the child grows up, he or she can in turn teach his or her child in a similar way so that good spiritual traditions can be propagated. Children learn by imitating and following the example of their parents. Besides an in-born natural disposition, the parents are an important factor in molding the character of the child. The sharing of suffering between parents and child creates a strong bond between them. Many parents complain in old age that their children do not care about them. This is because the parents have not shown that example of caring for their grand-parents in the first place.

To forge a bond and a deep relationship, the parent must have three things: first, love and concern in the Lord for the child; second, proper discipline and chastisement and the showing of parental example; and third, sharing of life's good, misfortune, happiness, and suffering.

The relationship and bond between husband and wife rest on two things: love and concern for each other in the spirit of selflessness and understanding and the bearing of one another's burdens and suffering despite incompatibilities.

Sharing in the church

Besides the fellowship of suffering within the family, there is also the fellowship of suffering with other members of the body of Christ. In the early church during the apostles' time, the believers simply sold all their possessions, brought the proceeds to the church, and distributed them among the poorer and more needy brethren. There was that feeling of "what I have is yours, and what you have I can have when I need it." There was mutual sharing of one another's goods in the church, and the church was actually one big family. The problems and suffering of one member were keenly felt by all other members. Whatever problem needed to be settled could be arbitrated in the presence of the apostles. The apostles became the fathers of the church family; and later on, when the load became too heavy, the task was passed to the seven deacons.

With the event of the martyrdom of Stephen and the beginning of the persecution of the church in Jerusalem, however, many of the Christians were scattered abroad. It then became difficult for Christians to share their wealth with others. Still, the sharing of joy and suffering continued on as before, as is evident in the Book of Acts and Paul's epistles. Not only were sufferings shared among early church Christians, but also the taking up of other people's allocation of suffering. Thus Paul in Colossians 1:24 said, "[I] who now rejoice in my suffering for you, and fill up that which is behind of the afflictions of Christ in my flesh for his body's sake, which is the church." It is as if God had purposed and imposed a certain amount of suffering for the body of Christ, so that collectively this amount of suffering has to be discharged. If you do not suffer a certain amount, other members of the body have to make up the difference. To be fair, of course, those who suffer more will get more spiritual benefit.

In the churches of today, however, there are many hurdles to this sharing of wealth, not to mention sharing of suffering. There are many reasons why it is difficult to carry out this process. Church members are not close enough in friendship to warrant willingness to share one another's wealth and suffering. In other words, one would not go out of one's way to sell one's house to help a friend or to make great sacrifices. There are so many disagreeable church members today. The memberships of the church are not properly screened: there are those that are not yet saved and who join the church as advantage seekers; there is not a long enough period of initiation and observation before admission; and the mobility of members is another discouraging factor.

When you help a friend, you expect that somehow he will be around when you need help — helping each other in turn with big favors. In some isolated rural and farming communities, where people stay in one place for many generations, favor and indebtedness carry down through generations. There is that sentiment of "because his father helped my father, I still owe him a favor; and if he is in trouble

I will help him." Charity, too, unconsciously becomes a kind of long-term investment, even though the motive for charity should be without any conditions and hope of return.

Without sharing of wealth, the sharing and fellowship of suffering can only be carried out to a certain degree. Real fellowship of suffering is sacrificial. If you really shared another person's suffering, you would be willing to help him financially. Fellowship of suffering is another form of love for one another. It is a condition for discipleship, because Christ said, "By this shall all men know that ye are my disciples, if ye have love one to another" (John 13:35).

Fellowship of Suffering with Christ

Having experienced the fellowship of suffering between members of the body of Christ, one should be ready to experience the fellowship of suffering with Christ. Suffering with Christ is a very abstract form of experience. We cannot explain and pinpoint the experience to nonbelievers, but for believers it is real and exists spiritually. It is just like a Christian's eternal life: you cannot feel it, nor can you prove it; it is something that you accept by faith. But the fellowship of suffering with Christ can equally be felt and experienced. Take the instance of being reviled and reproached because of your belief, because of Christ. Romans 15:3 says, "The reproaches of them that reproached thee fell on me." It is Christ that feels about it the most. Here on earth you feel about it too: you feel it the way Christ feels about it, minus the feeling of the flesh, plus Christ's love. What this means is that you may feel what Christ feels in a way, but you have something else that Christ does not feel: that feeling of human hatred of the flesh and that lacking of the love and forgiveness of Christ. When Christ was reviled, he still had compassion for his enemies and forgave them. But for us, the feeling of the flesh is anger, hatred, and vindication, not to mention revenge. All these do not apply to Christ. So you have to be quite spiritual to feel the way Christ feels. Our ego and self often alter the godly feelings. A spiritual man is one who has mortified the deeds of the body, buffeted the flesh and brought it into subjection, and now walks after the Spirit. Only thus conditioned would one be able to feel more closely what Christ feels.

49

However, what is most difficult to explain is the experience of suffering with Christ on the cross. The consummation of a person's spiritual experience is found in Philippians 3:10-11: "That I may know him, and the power of his resurrection, and the fellowship of his sufferings, being made conformable unto his death; if by any means I might attain unto the resurrection of the dead." How do we feel it? Take the example of breaking bread (Holy Communion) in a church where everyone gets together, shares with each other verses of the Scripture and their feelings about the suffering of Christ, prays together, and then finally breaks bread. Let us say we do it every day in our own home with family and friends, just like in the early church — worshipping together in the temple, going through the nearly daily experience of suffering for the gospel, and sharing the suffering between brethren. Then we would begin to experience that spiritual experience of participating in Christ's suffering and death.

The Virgin Mary

Of all the women God created, none has received more grace from God than the Virgin Mary. God bestowed so much grace on her that her heart leaped in joy and ecstasy: "My spirit hath rejoiced in God my Savior" (Luke 1:47). As was the extra portion of grace that she had received, so God had exacted from her that extra portion of fellowship of suffering with Christ. The prophet Simeon, who was in the temple at the time of presentation of the child Christ, prophesied to Mary, "Yea, a sword shall pierce through thy own soul also" (Luke 2:35). To Mary the suffering of Christ was as painful as a sword piercing through her heart. She had that deep sense of suffering with Christ. The Scripture referred to her as "blessed" (Luke 1:48), not only because she was the mother of Jesus in the flesh, but also because she suffered with Christ.

Comfort Each Other

God lets us suffer so that we may comfort those who suffer. Only those who have had the same sickness understand the pain of that sickness and those who suffer from it. So only those who have suffered can comfort those who suffer. Those who have suffered can become a blessing to others. When I suffer, I feel lost until someone who has suffered the same thing comes to comfort me because he has been through the same thing.

Paul, in the first chapter of Second Corinthians, has profoundly shared with us the mystery of the fellowship of suffering. He witnessed God's hand of comfort in all our suffering: when we suffer God comforts (1:4), though we may not be aware of it oftentimes. If God does not comfort, what would become of us? We would despair much more and give up. That we are able to endure our suffering is already a proof that God has comforted us by giving us the strength to endure. So the beautiful purpose of God in letting us suffer and comforting us while we suffer is that we may in turn be comforters to those who suffer. Yes, God wants us to propagate this beneficial chain of comfort among the members of the body of Christ. This is an example of the fellowship of suffering in Christ.

Then Paul goes further into the meaning of suffering in verse 5. He says, "For as the sufferings of Christ abound in us, so our consolation also aboundeth by Christ." Why does Paul suddenly switch from our suffering to the suffering of Christ? The true meaning of suffering can only be found in Christ. If we were to look into the Scriptures, especially the portion on the prayer of Christ in the Garden of Gethsemane, we would see that Christ suffered because he was obedient to God. He suffered to fulfill the will of the Father. Because of his suffering and death, we are saved. Therefore, true suffering in the sight of God can only be found in obedience to God and, strictly speaking, only in Christ. God delights only in the merits of the suffering and obedience of his Son Jesus Christ. This is why he has given his Son a name that is above every name.

God wants to make our suffering of eternal significance by placing our suffering in Christ. He even bestowed upon us the privilege of having the suffering of Christ when we suffer in accordance to his will. This is why Paul said that the "suffering of Christ aboundeth in us." Furthermore, he said, "so our consolation also aboundeth by Christ." Since our suffering in Christ is the suffering of Christ, it follows that any comfort derived from it is the consolation of Christ. Yes, all consolation comes from Christ when we suffer in him. This is the true meaning of comfort in Christ.

Finally, Paul expounded this mystery of suffering in Christ by revealing to us that his suffering is part of his walk with God. As Paul walks with God, he walks in affliction, so that it will work out to be consolation and salvation to the Corinthians. That is to say, by so doing, he leads more Corinthians to the saving knowledge of Christ. Suffering is so intimately bound up with Paul's walk with God that he takes it to be the necessary and prime element in his ministry. By going through all these sufferings, Paul is able to be used of God as an instrument of consolation. Moreover, God reckons his suffering in Christ as merits and thus gives consolation by measure to those to whom Paul ministers.

Paul would therefore want the Corinthians to reckon their suffering to be in Christ as they are the partakers of the suffering (verse 7), so that, like Paul, they will receive the consolation of God.

Let's Cry Together

We live in a he-man world where people say that those who cry are weaklings. So we go through life with clenched fists, pent-up emotions, and cooked-up resentment.

Modern people, living in a modern society, have lost the art of crying together. In the Old Testament the Jews mourned whenever their family, friends, and honored personalities died. Whenever they had done wrong and repented, they mourned. When they were in difficulties and sufferings, they cried.

Crying on each other's shoulders with fellow sufferers produces that sympathy link and fellowship bond that no amount of words of comfort can produce. You cannot get close to a man's heart unless you cry with him. This is why the apostle Paul said in Romans 12:15, "Rejoice with them that do rejoice, and weep with them that weep." Sisters are often more adept at this than brothers.

God Hears

Have you ever experienced praying to God over and over again and yet nothing happens until you feel so desperate that you cry and something happens? God knows our miseries and hears our cries. When the Israelites were in Egypt suffering greatly under the oppression of their taskmasters, they cried to God; and God heard them by sending Moses to lead them out of Egypt. It was Dr. Engstrom who said, "As we suffer, we need to know that we are welcome to cry at the feet of Jesus. He himself will cry with us — a cry of pain, a cry of compassion, a cry of understanding — indeed a cry that calls forth a new morning."

The Pinnacle of Spirituality

As we suffer and grow in Christ, we enter into deeper relationship with God. The Scripture calls this "knowing God." As God dwells in us and we in him, we will know the Father and the Holy Spirit through the Lord Jesus. The Holy Spirit will open our hearts and our understanding so that we may know God and enter into the fellowship of the Trinity. The knowledge of the Trinity and the fellowship with the Trinity will enable us to walk with God and dwell in the secret fellowship of the Trinity — this is what is meant by "dwelling in the secret place of the Most High." It is the pinnacle of spirituality of a Christian. The gateway to the pinnacle of spirituality is utter obedience to God, utter self-abasement, and then going through suffering with Christ.

Deliverance from Sin
unto Sanctification

Chapter 6

Suffering as the Result of Our Sins

Whose Fault?

As we dwell more on suffering, we are hard pressed to find a way to distinguish between suffering that comes to us through no fault of our own and suffering that comes to us because of our own faults and inadequacies.

If you look at all the Christians around you, you might somehow feel that a lot of suffering could be due to their own faults. Even in a perfect environment, one still gets into trouble and suffering. Human nature is intrinsically that way for many of us. Even in a sinless state, man still yields to temptation and gets into trouble. Look at Adam, who lived in the beautiful garden of Eden and was the ruler of all the creatures on earth. He was sinless, albeit innocent. Yet he succumbed to temptation and plunged himself into sin, suffering, and death. Not contented with what he had, he wanted to be like God in knowledge. Paul said in 1 Timothy 6:6, "But godliness with contentment is great gain." If only Adam had had the Bible to remind him! We now have the Bible, yet we often take it for granted. Perhaps too, like the brothers in Christ's parable of Lazarus and the rich man, who had the law of Moses and the prophets to listen to, Adam had God's commandment, so that if he did not heed it, then any amount of Scripture would have been of no avail in keeping him from falling. It is a pity that even though many of us suffer because of our faults, prejudices, bad personalities, habits, and sentiments, we will still never listen and never learn. There is a Chinese saying that goes like this: "There is no remedy for those who deliberately sin against themselves." So let us dwell on those who are willing to listen.

When It Serves Us Right

Even as children of God, we have occasions to do wrong; and when it happens, we receive the suffering that is the result of it. One may ask, When I do wrong purposely and suffer for it, it serves me right; but when I do wrong inadvertently, or when I am dragged into it without choice, am I also responsible for it? In real-life situations it is difficult to assess the cause by the effects. Besides, it may plunge one into endless introspection. But one thing we know is that some-where along the line we have done something wrong. Confess that before God. Be humble and ready to admit your wrong and ask for God's forgiveness. If you are innocent and go about confessing what you consider to be a fault, God will not consider you guilty just because you admit guilt. In this world's court, if you admit guilt when you are innocent, you fall into the danger of being pronounced guilty by the jury and the judge because nobody in this world can read another's mind. God is different: he sees not as man sees. He is the sole justifier of humanity. But if one tries to justify oneself, then one would fall into the danger of unconfessed sins.

When suffering comes, take it with a positive mind; solve and remedy the problem; do full restitution on it; and, above all, confess everything before God. Learn your lessons the hard way. You must be determined to let this happening be the first and the last time: never do it again for the rest of your life. (Even though in reality you may still do it again, this should not alter your frame of mind in this matter.) All this must be done with a sense of trusting God to work through you to do it, not by trusting the strength or the capability of the flesh. It is just like saying, "By the grace of God I won't repeat the same mistake again."

God's Provision for Cleansing

When we accept Christ as our Savior and confess that we are sinners, Christ forgives all our past sins. We do not need to spend months digging out our past sins and confessing each of them one by one. After we become Christians, if we commit sins and confess them before God and ask for forgiveness, the sin that we are not conscious of or that we overlook to confess (not willfully, of course), God takes care of also. It is automatically forgiven — forgiven even though we are not conscious of it. But for this there are certain requirements.

God has already provided a way, a scheme, you might call it, whereby you can be cleansed of sins committed unawares in your daily life. 1 John 1:7 says, "But if we walk in the light, as he is in the light, we have fellowship with one another, and the blood of Jesus Christ his Son cleanseth us from all sin." Then verse 9 goes on to say, "If we confess our sins, he is faithful and just to forgive us our sins, and to cleanse us from all unrighteousness." There are two conditions that qualify us for cleansing of sins. First, we must walk in the light, which means we must not live a life of sin, but instead live a life that is consistent with what Christ has lived as our example. Second, we must have fellowship with one another, which means to live in harmony with one another. Yes, the word *fellowship* has many connotations: it means close relationship, mutual help and sharing, mutual exhortation, prayer, helping and loving one another. If we do all these, then the sins we have committed unconsciously will be already cleansed by the blood of Christ. This we also find in the Old Testament. "Who can understand his errors? cleanse thou me from secret faults" (Ps. 19:12). There are times when we do not realize we have errors and sins, but God has already forgiven us. The sins we have committed and know about, we confess and God forgives.

There are some schools of Christian counseling that advocate counseling with Christians who have problems and hangovers from the past to dig out their past unpleasant experiences and deal with them. This is very much like modern psychiatry. As for myself, I had a lot of hurts in my past, but when I firmly believed that God forgives, they simply vanished like a mist. The secret is that when God forgives, I must also forgive: I must be reconciled with my mean enemy. As for myself, by the grace of God, as far as I am aware, I have no human enemy. There may be someone who hates me, but I do not hate him, and I do not consider myself his enemy. I have to, because if I had less forgiveness and love, I would have ended up on a Christian counselor's couch. The only enemy I have to watch out for is Satan, who is like a roaring lion.

David's Experience

What is the biblical example of forgiveness of sin unaware? It is found in the life of David. When David had committed adultery with Bathsheba and caused her to be pregnant, he wanted to cover up the matter. David persuaded her husband Uriah to go back home and pass the night with her. But Uriah, being a faithful captain and loyal to his commission, would rather abide with his soldiers during the night before the battle than go back home and have pleasure with his wife. So David, not being able to cover up the matter, had no choice but to order his general Joab to send Uriah to the most dangerous position in the front line so as to have him killed in battle. It worked, and Uriah was killed. David had used one evil to cover up another. In a way he was dragged into doing another evil, after he had done the first one.

When Nathan the prophet, who had a close relationship with David, came and pointed out his sins, David said, "I have sinned against the Lord" (2 Sam. 12:13). And Nathan said to David, "The Lord hath also put away thy sin; thou shalt not die." David was a man of God and always walked in the light; David and Nathan had close fellowship with one another and were free to point out each other's faults and sins. It might even be that Nathan, knowing David's sins, had interceded for him. But most important, God wanted to forgive David.

Confession Is No Merit by Itself

Remember that confession, like faith, is not a work or merit that warrants the forgiveness of God. For we ourselves have not paid the price for our sins. It is only by an appeal to God, the justifier of man, to have mercy on us that we receive forgiveness of our sins. God's forgiveness is a free gift; we do not earn it with our confession.

Confessing our sins and God's forgiving is the rule, but the exception is that God also forgives whomsoever he will, regardless of whether he or she has consciously asked for it. The man sick of palsy in Matthew 9:2 had his sins forgiven, not because he confessed or asked for it, but because Jesus had seen the faith of the men who brought him there. It may or may not have even been the faith of the man with the palsy.

The adulteress caught in the act was brought before Jesus, and Jesus was confronted with the question whether or not she should be stoned. In his wisdom, Jesus answered that those who had no sin should cast the first stone. Everyone was convicted in their consciences, so they left the woman and Jesus alone. Jesus' final words were, "Neither do I condemn thee: go, and sin no more" (John 8:11). When Jesus said that he would not condemn her, it meant that God had forgiven her sins; otherwise by God's law she must die. "The soul that sinneth, it shall die" (Ezek. 18:4). In the context of John's Gospel, there was silence on the part of both Jesus and the woman except for what was recorded in the passage. So apparently she did not confess her sins. According to Moses' law, when she sinned, there was no way out except waiting for death; no amount of confession would secure her acquittal. The woman knew that confession wouldn't help. But in his mercy, Jesus forgave her regardless. (In Christ's time the right of capital punishment was taken away from the Sanhedrin, the assembly, and the court of Moses' law and replaced by the Roman law. This was why the Sanhedrin wanted Pontius Pilate the governor to sentence Jesus to death. However, there were cases of capital punishment being taken into the hands of Jews for breaking Moses' law — just like lynching.)

Some biblical expositors maintain that God forgave David's sins the moment he confessed before Nathan. If David had said, "I am confessing my sins," and Nathan had replied, "God now forgives your sins," then what these expositors have said would be correct. However, if we examine the time frame in the context of the passage, it is otherwise. When David said, "I have sinned against the Lord," it means David admitted committing adultery with Bathsheba and causing Uriah's death. It was a past happening. When Nathan replied, "The Lord hath also put away thy sin; thou shalt not die" (2 Sam. 12:13), it referred to the same time frame in the past. *Hath also* implies "in addition, following closely after this event." Both are past happenings, one following another. So it means, "You had sinned at that time, but God had forgiven you then and there. If God did not forgive your sins you would have to die because of them." For the present, David had to realize them, repent of them, confess them, and face God's punishment and consequences.

David, being a man after God's heart, had known quite well what was right and what was wrong. Yet it seemed David had a moral blind spot in this matter. He was so preoccupied with solving the problem of coverup that after all was resolved, he had somehow forgotten or missed the fact that he had done great wrong. To David it became a secret fault, otherwise, as a godly man, he would have repented in sackcloth and ashes. So God had to send the prophet Nathan to point out the sin to David. God wanted David to know, to confess, and to repent. Nevertheless, God had already forgiven David because he was not aware of it. David repented for a long time afterwards and wrote Psalm 51 and other psalms of repentance.

God Forgives Sins but not the Consequences

When God forgives our sins, it does not necessarily mean that God will waive the consequence of sin, nor does God exempt us from the suffering that derives from it. We can see this in the life of David, his beloved saint. Though God forgave David's sins, he did not exempt him from chastisement: he dealt severely with his sins. He put David in open shame before the people of Israel to teach them that not even a king, the anointed of the Lord, even the beloved of the Lord, could get away with adultery and murder. He meted out his punishment to David by decreeing that the sword would never depart from his house; his wives would be defiled in the same way that he defiled another person's wife. David suffered much because of the sins he had committed, and God did not make life easier for him even though he was a man after God's own heart.

Yes, God's punishment and chastisement are the heaviest for those he loves the most; and the more he loves, the more the suffering. Look at Christ: he is the most beloved of God, and yet he suffered most, not because he had done any wrong but because he had to bear the wrongs and sins of all humanity on the cross. Let us not compare our suffering with that of our brothers and sisters or ask God why they can get away so lightly.

The Most Poignant Confession

But David did not take God's forgiveness for granted. He afterwards repented exceedingly. It was with great sorrow that he wrote Psalm 51, the most moving piece of confession of sins written by man to God. If you were to ask me how I feel about the whole confession, I would say:

What
an appeal to God's mercy and tenderness
What
a remorse of heart
What
sadness it is for a man to feel
he has let God down
Whereas
God had considered him to be
a man after his own heart
Yet
he did exactly the opposite
What
a disappointment to God,
and what can David say now?
What
a poignancy of speech
What
a desire to be cleansed
What
helplessness!
There is
nothing that David could sacrifice
to atone for his sins
There is
nothing that a man can give to God
in return for his grace and mercy
Except contrition of heart.

Craving for Suffering

Let us look at the life of the apostle Paul. Before his conversion he greatly persecuted the church. After his conversion, he was the apostle who endured the most persecution. Whereas before his conversion he persecuted the church, after his conversion he was persecuted in exactly the same way. It was as if the suffering that Paul endured was a restitution for his past atrocities, though God had forgiven all his sins when he was converted. If we read between the lines in the Book of Acts, we almost feel that Paul preferred the route of suffering. It seems that he wanted to make up for what he had done as the chief of sinners. He was forbidden by the Holy Spirit through the disciples, Philip's daughters, and the prophet Agabus to go to Jerusalem (Acts 21:4). Yet Paul persisted despite all of these warnings, and God finally allowed it and gave him assurance. It seems that God had been gracious in allowing Paul the choice of an easier and less persecuted life, but Paul wanted to take one that entailed more suffering.

Peter's Repentance

Latin church tradition has the legend that the apostle Peter, after denying Christ three times, felt so sorry afterwards, even after Christ's ascension and after Pentecost, that he wept exceedingly for two years. He wept so much that his tears ate into his lower eyelids and made pockets in them. All his life he wanted to make up for his denial of Christ, and he chose a more severe martyrdom by requesting his executors to nail him on the cross upside-down, because he felt he was not worthy of dying like Christ.

By far the most worthless suffering of a Christian is for the sins he has committed. It is the suffering that fits into the saying: "you asked for it." Since a Christian has to go through suffering all his life, it would be much better and wiser to do good and suffer, than to do evil and suffer. We all have to suffer one way or another, so why don't we suffer for doing good? 1 Peter 3:17 says, "For it is better, if the will of God be so, that ye suffer for well doing, than for evil doing." Peter, like Paul, had comprehended the great merits of suffering; his epistle reads like the apologetics of suffering.

The Corinthians' Repentance

Much can be learned from our suffering, even though it is due to our own faults. Suffering brings us back to self-examination; it makes us realize where we have gone wrong and leads us to godly repentance. When Paul was dealing with some of the problems of the church at Corinth, he wrote First Corinthians to point out the blatant mistakes and the great sins of adultery in the church. When the Christians in the church at Corinth heard of it, they were sorrowful and repentant. Paul was satisfied with their genuineness; and in his moment of tenderness, he felt that he had been somewhat too harsh on them, like a father beating his child too hard for wrongdoing and feeling sorry afterwards. So he wrote Second Corinthians to comfort them, cuddle them, and assure them that they were on the right track. 2 Corinthians 7:9-12 bears testimony to the fact that there existed between Paul and the Corinthians that fellowship of joy, sorrow, and suffering. When the Corinthians sinned and suffered, Paul suffered also. He was very concerned about their well-being and genuinely shared their suffering. He felt just like parents who have heartaches when their children do wrong. When they did not please God in their living, Paul was very disturbed, impatient, and indignant; and that made him suffer even more.

What Father Likes Best

When you have a child who is full of mischief and often gets himself into trouble, you want to discipline him. Sometimes he is so naughty and boisterous that you have to keep on spanking him — even though spanking does not quiet him for long. You feel so frustrated and you almost think there is no cure. Then suddenly, in a moment of sensibility, he comes to you with a sorry and abject look. He confesses his wrongs profusely, and immediately it melts your heart; you feel that he is the most lovely child in all the world. You almost want to tell him that you are ready to forget all his wrongdoings and admonish him to start all over again as a good boy. Yes, this is the soft spot of most parents.

God in the Old Testament provided ordinances of sacrifice as atonement for sin committed. The Jew who had done wrong had to make sacrifices to become right with God, that is, at peace with him. Yet David, who was a man after God's heart and knew God's mind, has given away God's soft spot when he says, in Psalm 51:16-17, "For thou desirest not sacrifice; else would I give it; thou delightest not in burnt offerings. The sacrifices of God are a broken spirit: a broken and a contrite heart, O God, thou wilt not despise."

Very often we confess our sin before God because we are told that this is what we should do. The Scripture says it, so we do it mechanically, like cleaning our dishes. The true saints of God have always keenly felt that they have deeply offended God himself, more than merely breaking some commandments. The saint comes to God in a humble way acknowledging God's righteousness and acknowledging how unrighteous he is. He comes to God desiring and entreating God to forget and to blot out his sins so that God will not remember them. He expresses great desire to be clothed with God's righteousness so that he may once more enter into the favor of God and be immersed in his grace and mercy.

Chapter 7

Suffering as a Weapon against Sin

The Most Powerful Weapon

The First Letter of Peter says explicitly that it is suffering that enables us to defend against and stay clear of sin. When we are armed with the weapon of suffering, we are able to keep ourselves from falling into the lusts of the flesh and sin. "Forasmuch then as Christ hath suffered for us in the flesh, arm yourselves likewise with the same mind: for he that hath suffered in the flesh hath ceased from sin; that he no longer should live the rest the rest of his time in the flesh to the lust of men, but to the will of God" (1 Peter 4:1-2). Much can be said about these two verses.

First, Christ is the pioneer and captain of our salvation. He came out victorious over sin and death by rising from the dead. He secured for us a victorious route, so that whoever treads the same route arrives at the same goal. So when we believe in Christ, we are walking the same route of death and resurrection. We too are victorious over death. No doubt many young Christians would say, "But I don't feel anything of death and certainly not of resurrection." Yes, all the spiritual battles are taking place in the high places in heaven, so we cannot see them, feel them, or hear about them except in the Bible. We have to accept it by faith. But it makes all the difference to us. The resurrection, which takes place in the last day, makes a great divide between Christians and non-Christians. The Christians go to eternal life and non-Christians to eternal death. It also makes a great difference on earth here and now. Those who are in Christ live a regenerated life, a life of faith, hope, and love — plus joy to go with it, even in suffering and death! Yes, you may not feel the effects of death and resurrection, but you already have experienced them and are even now living a life to that effect.

Second, just as we believe by faith that Christ died and rose from the dead to secure a new life for us, we also take by faith the suffering of Christ to deal with our sins. When we go through suffering, we identify our suffering with the suffering of Christ so that we get the benefit of our sins being put away. Suffering is therefore our weapon against sin. How effective is our weapon? It is as effective as Christ's suffering in dealing with our sins; and certainly that is more than enough for us.

Christians Must Go the Hard Way

The Christian route in life is often the most difficult. We have to pay a price and suffer disadvantage, but it is Christ's way. It is when we want an easy way out, shortcuts, quick ways to make money, and the way of pleasure and ease that we get ourselves trapped in sin. All the great saints of God had hard and difficult lives. They could have chosen an easier life, but they preferred the way of suffering. Meditate on what Jesus said: "Enter ye in at the strait gate: for wide is the gate, and broad is the way, that leadeth to destruction, and many there be which go in thereat: Because strait is the gate, and narrow is the way, which leadeth unto life, and few there be that find it" (Matt. 7:13-14).

When we go through suffering for righteousness, for what is sacrificial, for giving love and benefit to our fellowman, we are in effect putting our faith in God's promise. Because we have trusted him, he will never let us down. Sometimes we may not see the immediate results in life, but we will surely see them and receive his reward when we see him in the life to come.

As we recall our past life of sin, we remember that when we sin, the effects of sin bring about suffering from which there is no hope or even benefits. If there were, then we would sin less and less as we learn our lessons. But the world has shown us that the human race never learns from its sins; instead, it goes on sinning more and more. Without the restraining work of God, the world will go into self-destruction very fast. It is by God's grace that he suffers our folly and gives us more time to repent before he closes in at the final reckoning, which is the fearful judgment of God.

The Saints' Experience

Joseph suffered under the hands of his brothers. They were jealous of him because he prophesied from his dreams that he would be ruling over them. The final provocation came when he visited his brothers in a beautiful, multicolored robe given to him by his father Jacob. They pounced on him, stripped off his robe, and cast him into a dry pit. He would have been killed had not Reuben and Judah intervened and delivered him out of the hands of his angry brothers. Instead, he was sold as a slave and brought to Egypt. He worked for Potiphar, Pharaoh's officer. When Potiphar's wife took an interest in him and tried to seduce him, he refused her because he was righteous and feared God. Failing to appropriate what she had lusted after, she maligned Joseph before her husband, and he was put into prison. Yes, Joseph suffered as the price of refusing to sin. Yet the prison became his route to glory. Pharaoh made him ruler of all Egypt because he was the only one who could interpret Pharaoh's dreams, and he therefore saved Egypt from starvation.

The prophet Daniel was thrown into the lions' den because he insisted on praying to God as many as three times a day. God vindicated his cause before King Darius by sealing the mouths of the lions.

John the Baptist was not afraid of speaking the truth and upholding the commandment of God. He rebuked Herod the tetrarch for taking his brother Philip's wife Herodias and for all the evils he had done; consequently, he was put into prison. Finally, he was beheaded because she wanted his head on a plate.

My Experience

I can still remember, when I was a shy little boy of twelve in school, the time that a lot of my classmates decided to cooperate in cheating on the exam by copying from each other, preparing answers and writing them down on their thighs. At that time we wore shorts, so every time someone pulled up the leg of his shorts we could see the answers. I disagreed, refused to cooperate with them in passing the answers to each other, and told them that it was blatant dishonesty. There was no one to stand by my side and take the same stand. My classmates literally pounced on me. For the whole school year I was ostracized, jeered at, and given the nickname "saint." For my tender boyish heart it was the whole world going against me, and it seemed that the whole roof had caved in. I went home often praying to God, "O God, do we Christians have to pay such a dear price in life?" Yes, in my suffering I have found that I became even more and more sensitive to other forms of dishonesty. I was strengthened further by suffering to take a harder stand against dishonesty. Since I had already paid my price in life, I might as well be honest all the way. Yes, through suffering I was freed from the sins of dishonesty.

Forty years later, my youngest son Aaron came to me sadly and said, "Dad, how come I am so different from most of my classmates, who lie and swear, and do not believe in God?" So I encouraged him: "That, my boy, is because you are a born-again Christian. Have nothing to do with dishonesty and lies. Hit back at them the way you hit your balls. Don't miss any of them!" He was the best batter on his baseball team.

The Merits of Christ's Suffering

When we sin, the harmful effects of sin remain, and something must be done to undo the effects of sin. In Exodus 22, God commanded the people of Israel to make restitution when they sinned. For example, if a person stole another man's cow or sold it, he would have to make restitution by paying back the owner five cows. Yes, when a man sinned, he made an offering for sin, and then he also made restitution to the person he had wronged.

Someone may ask: What about Adam's sin in us — the original sin we all inherit from Adam? How do we make restitution for our original sin after we have accepted Christ and are saved? Do we humans have the capability of making restitution to God for the disobedience to God in the Garden of Eden? What can we do? There is nothing that we can do. But God has a way.

The suffering and death of Christ are always mentioned in conjunction with each other. Not much has been said about suffering as it stands alone. I have given much thought to the suffering of Christ; and the more I think about it, the more I am led to believe that Christ's suffering on the cross deals with the effects of sin and hence its restitution. When a person sins, it results in afflictions, shame, reproach, and suffering. Christ in his suffering has borne our shame and reproach. Christ's death on the cross takes care of our penalty for sin and death. Christ suffering on the cross dealt with restitution for sin and the effects of sin. Why are the effects of sin detrimental? Satan is constantly accusing us before God, so we must get rid of the bad effects of sin, by faith through the suffering of Christ.

There are, however, the dangerous and indelible effects of sin in life that we must avoid. Let us take the example of sexual sins. Once you have contracted venereal disease, it is difficult to get healed. At present there is no cure for AIDS. Yes, you may come to God and repent, become a very good Christian, on fire for God, but the effect of sin stays with you. There is a saying which goes: "God may forgive your sins, but your body won't!" In 1 Corinthians 6:18 we read: "Every sin that man doeth is without the body; but he that committeth fornication sinneth against his own body." Yes, sinning against one's body is the "AIDS" of sin.

God has accomplished his work of redemption through the cross of Christ. God has dealt with it down to the last detail. When Christ cried "It is finished," his work of redemption was done. We cannot do anything more to enhance his work. All we can do is to accept it by faith.

By Faith

In the course of Christian living there is suffering. We should take it with faith and joy, for we are in effect suffering in a vicarious way the suffering of Christ on the cross. In our suffering God reminds us that Christ has resisted sin to the extent of suffering and death. We must remember it all the time lest we become weary and discouraged. Yes, enduring suffering give us the strength to resist sins. It is our weapon against sin; not that we are able to resist sin by ourselves, but that Christ has been victorious in resisting sin through suffering. So by faith in Christ, we are in fellowship with his suffering and can resist sins.

71

My Reckoning Experience

Specific reckoning in suffering and suffering with reckoning is the most effective way of ridding us of sinful habits and habits of committing sin. Reckoning is a spiritual step and stand that we take in cutting off all our connections with sin and living in the light of this new stand. In Romans 6, Paul tells us that as Christians we are baptized into Christ's death, burial, and resurrection; therefore our old man has already been crucified with him. To put our new spiritual status into living reality, Paul teaches us to "Likewise reckon ye also yourselves to be dead indeed unto sin, but alive unto God through Jesus Christ our Lord" (Rom. 6:11).

Reckoning is a very powerful spiritual measure and step, but it also takes great faith, without the slightest doubt, otherwise it won't work. Watchman Nee, in his book *Normal Christian Life,* said that he tried reckoning for a long time, but it did not work until one day the Holy Spirit brought him to the realization of what reckoning is. Then it worked, and he was delivered from a lot of sins. Unfortunately he did not relate in detail to posterity what the realization was and how it was brought about.

I too did a lot of reckoning for years, and still my sinful habits were not completely or even mostly rid of until the Holy Spirit gave me further realization. It was a great improvement, but still I had some residual problems. Then persecution and suffering came. When I prayed to God in desperation, I learned to assert Christ's lordship in my life and my total commitment to him in a more thorough way, and then do my reckoning. It worked; a lot of vices disappeared overnight. I feel that I am a newer Christian. I don't know why I am so different now. It does not mean that I do not sin anymore, but it does mean that the little sin that bothers me and those that I have previously not been able to conquer can now be overcome. Having been rid of small sins, I will then be able to uncover smaller and smaller sins, which will become my next concern. Previously I was not consciously aware of these smaller and smaller sins. As we grow and walk in the Spirit, our spiritual discernment becomes more and more sensitive, and smaller and smaller sins come to our notice. Having won the battle of the small batch of sins, the next battle will be the smaller and smaller batch of sins. The spiritual battle goes on and on.

Once we have thus overcome the smaller and smaller habitual sins, there is still another form of sin that we should always be cautious about. It is the sudden temptation which comes to us in a moment we are not watchful. When it strikes, it strikes suddenly — and we are caught unaware. King David was a man after God's heart and walked perfectly before God, yet he could not defend himself from the sudden temptation of Bathsheba.

All this does not mean that we encounter the experience of the situation of Romans 7, where the things that we want to do we cannot do, and the things we do not wish to do, we do against our own will. It is a totally different situation. Yes, there is even more sensitivity to sin and the slightest faults, but it does not cause self-accusations and agony like that in Romans 7. Instead, it increases our confidence to accept suffering and by God's grace and strife to gain higher moral ground and goals. We have overcome and conquered, but we have not won the war until the day we see the Lord. Then there will be no more battles and suffering. God will give us a glorious body and we shall be like him: glorious and sinless.

I tried to analyze the steps logically and theologically so that I could share with other Christians how to do it; however, I still cannot describe in a way that is understood by all the basic requirement, which is the state of dedication to God. I guess the transformation of life in the Spirit is beyond the human mind. All I can say is that the few months of suffering have been able to accomplish for me what I could not achieve in many years. Reckoning is not a single incident; it is more of a realization of how our entire spiritual status, as described in Romans 6, 7, and 8, fits together. Reckoning is like a string: it strings together all the pearls in chapters 6, 7, and 8 to form a beautiful spiritual pearl necklace. Further discussion is beyond the scope of this book; God willing, I could share with you in detail in another book.

1 Peter 4:1 says, "For he that hath suffered in the flesh hath ceased from sin." Therefore, we must reckon the merits of suffering in overcoming sins. Do your Christian disciplines. They will work wonderfully. Once you have experienced them, you will be convinced that our old man has already been crucified and is completely dead and that we can be delivered from the struggles of the two laws in Romans 7. Victorious life can be a reality.

Chapter 8

Suffering as the Route
to Holiness

Christ's Example

Hebrews 13:12 says, "Wherefore Jesus also, that he might sanctify the people with his own blood, suffered without the gate." This is what Jesus Christ did. But what should we do? First Peter 2:21 says, "Christ also suffered for us, leaving us an example, that ye should follow his steps." First Peter 4:1 adds, "Forasmuch then as Christ hath suffered for us in the flesh, arm yourselves likewise with the same mind: for he that hath suffered in the flesh hath ceased from sin." Hebrews 12:10 also states that when God chastises us with suffering, it is for our profit, that we may be partakers of his holiness. The word *holiness* in most parts of the New Testament is rendered "Sanctification." It means we are specially separated to God and manifest a conduct compatible with the state we are in. Holiness is also an absolute quality of God: "partakers of his holiness."

Holiness as Separation

Let us first dwell on the meaning of *separation*. Take, for example, the food we eat. Food in cans can be kept for a long time without going bad and even without refrigeration. The food is cooked (sterilized) and then prevented from being contaminated with germs from the outside world, by being kept in sealed tin cans. Here we see the idea of separation and protection from contamination.

The whole world is being defiled or contaminated with evil. When God has chosen a people who is to be holy for himself, he separates them from the rest of the world. Without separation, his chosen people would get contaminated and fall into sin in this age of grace. We are separated, not so much physically but spiritually, from the rest of the unbelieving world, so that we can live our lives in holiness. When we are separated to God, we belong to him. But how can we belong to him if we are not holy? Therefore God also gives us his holiness by virtue of the blood of Jesus Christ which sanctifies us; that is to say, it makes us holy.

The world will always be against our moral separation from them. The world will not like us; they will consider us their enemies because they hate Christ in the first place. Suffering because of holiness will be the price we pay.

When you take the holy way in life, the world will give you a difficult road to walk on. The world will not appreciate you because you are righteous and good, kind and loving, but will instead try to take advantage of you.

Satan's Antagonism

We are runners in the race of life, who are being watched by spectators of this world and by principalities and powers in high places. These spectators are not our cheerleaders; instead, they are the scoffers: they don't want to see us winning the race. It is their hero and idols that they are cheering. Do not expect any cheering from the world. If the world does cheer you, take a very careful look at yourself: something must have gone wrong in you!

Have you ever experienced antagonism against Christians — that a person who consciously hates Christ will hate you also? Even in a strange and unfamiliar place, where everybody is a stranger to you, there comes someone who does something to your hurt, and that person does not even know that you are a Christian. Down through history there have been politicians who unconsciously made policies that really hurt Christians. These are the works of Satan, who uses human hands to carry out his tasks, whether consciously or unconsciously. Sometimes Satan gives people of the world the super-natural sense of being able to "sniff out," to choose Christians, and even persecute them, even without knowing them to be Christians.

The apostle Paul, before he was converted, searched and hunted around for Christians and committed them to prison. This is why Christ said, "If the world hate you, ye know that it hated me before it hated you. If ye were of the world, the world would love his own: but because ye are not of the world, but I have chosen you out of the world, therefore the world hateth you" (John 15:18-19).

The people of the world, the children of Satan, conspire to work against Christians. Satan manipulates situations and even disturbs nature to bring about harm to Christians. It is a system — a spiritually organized evil — that endeavors to destroy the work of the church and harass Christians. Its aim is to usurp the power of God in this world, to put into action the power of the Antichrist, and to build up his kingdom on earth so that his plan of usurping the world of God may be carried out, because in the latter days Satan, that Great Dragon, shall be cast down onto the earth (Rev. 12:9).

It is important, therefore, for Christians to beware of the mental attitude that has enslaved the people of this world and to overcome it: "Casting down imaginations, and every high thing that exalteth itself against the knowledge of God, and bringing into captivity every thought to the obedience of Christ" (2 Cor. 10:5).

Satan's Temptation

Let us dwell on holy living. Satan is bent on persecuting Christians who walk the path of holy living. He tries to make it more difficult for them to walk. He will tempt them with easy money, fame, and sex; he will set a trap in what seems to be legitimate and morally right: achievement, work satisfaction, and recognition from the world. It is not that these goals are not good in themselves, but if these goals produce the effect of drawing us away from holy living, then they are a trap for us. On the other hand, if Christ is our Lord and we walk according to his directive and will, then the same goals will even produce more spiritual benefits to us.

How to Discern

How do we distinguish the subtle differences above? Here are some of the guidelines to consider:

a) If we start out doing something to fulfill the aspirations of the flesh, the cravings and lust of our being, then we will end up with fruits which are bound to be perishable. "For he that soweth to his flesh shall of the flesh reap corruption, but he that soweth to the spirit shall of the spirit reap life everlasting." Our motive must be for God and from God.

b) Even when you do something which seemingly is for God but you do it by relying on your own strength, then you lose the spiritual blessings which would be yours had you done it by the power of the Holy Spirit.

c) While you are doing these things, who is your Lord all along? Is it a fulfillment of God's will? Or is it your will? Yes, very often in life you may be doing the right thing, but it is the wrong job for you. Read the incident recorded in 1 Chronicles 13:9, which depicts the journey of the God's Ark of the Covenant. Along the way the oxen stumbled, and it seemed imminent that the ark would fall out of the cart. Uzza, who was not a Levite, put out his hand to hold it and prevent it from falling. God was angry and killed him instantly, because God had specifically decreed that only people of the tribe of Levi could touch it. Uzza was doing the right thing, but unfortunately it was not his job. In our day, you can see examples in the military. There are many right things you can do, but if you do important tasks of your own accord without orders from your supervisor, you could be court-martialed.

When you are on the path of holiness, you will suffer. God allows suffering to come to you to keep you on the right path. Satan inflicts suffering and difficulties to discourage you from taking the right path. If you are afraid of suffering, you will fall prey to Satan's easy path. Satan will promise you an easy life and comfort, but God wants you to walk a difficult path.

Suffering as the route to holiness is contrary to human reasoning. In this age of science and technology, there are lots of inventions and gadgets to make life easy. There are myriads of pain killers to take the pain out of sicknesses. Health foods are more palatable than they used to be. Everything that is bitter is sugar-coated. No doubt it is difficult for a lot of non-Christian to understand suffering as something good.

The Cure

In the Eastern culture, where people take herbal medicines, they think differently. The herbs are boiled and cooked for hours like stew. The greater the illness, the more bitter the medicine. The medicine does not look good either. For example, the molt of the cicada looks exactly like a cockroach. The whole pot of medicine not only tastes bitter, but looks awful too! So the Chinese saying goes, "Bitter medicine is good for curing your illness." Then there is a famous saying which goes like this: "Before heaven entrusts a man with great responsibilities, it must first grieve his heart and mind; tax and labor his bones and sinews." So when a Chinese Christian suffers and you tell him that heaven is preparing him for a great task, he will accept it with gladness. Our spiritual sickness is sin influencing and getting into our life; and we must get rid of our spiritual sickness by spiritual medicine, which is suffering. It will look awful and taste bitter, but it will be good for curing sickness. Suffering will keep us and separate us away from sin and the influence of sin. "Wherefore come out from among them, and be ye separate, saith the Lord, and touch not the unclean thing, and I will receive you, and will be a Father unto you, and ye shall be my sons and daughters, saith the Lord Almighty" (2 Cor. 6:17-18).

Lot's Tragedy

The servants of Abraham and Lot had conflicts; they were squabbling for good pastures for their flocks. Finally they broke up. Lot had the priority of choosing the fertile plain of Sodom and Gomorra. At first Lot pitched his tent towards Sodom. Then, attracted by its materialistic abundance, he moved closer and closer until he came to dwell in the city. Then came the four kings who conquered the five kings of the plain city around Sodom and took Lot captive also. It took Abraham and his 318 well-trained servant fighters to rescue him. Still Lot did not move out of Sodom and come out from among his evil neighbors. Then God purposed to destroy Sodom and Gomorra. It took God's two angels to drag him and his family out of Sodom to escape from the rains of fire and brimstone from heaven. Still Lot's wife would not turn her eyes away from looking back at her possessions in Sodom — against the warning of the angels. She looked back and was turned into a pillar of salt. It was a tragic end for a family who knew God, who walked in righteousness (2 Peter 2:7), but who simply loved the world too much.

This is why Christ told the rich young ruler, who walked in the ways of God, keeping God's commandments, to sell all that he had, to give it to the poor, and then to follow Christ. But the rich young ruler loved the riches of this world more than Christ. He walked away in sadness. People who love the things of this world more than Christ will likewise eventually walk away from God in sadness.

The fear of abandonment of one's riches and the fear of following Christ arise from the need to cater to one's physical needs. It is also our entrenched notion of God wanting us to go the route of poverty, which many of the saints of God delight to take, to bear witness to God's sufficiency and provisions. However, more subtle than this fear is the tending, the catering to one's self and one's own ego. Poverty and need hurt one's ego.

Self Is Our Hurdle

Our self and ego loom much higher than we realize. Self is the biggest hurdle to holiness. Before we are saved, we have our system of actions and justification. We want to be righteous by ourselves. We set up a system of rules and then say to ourselves, "If I fulfill all these, then I should be called righteous." We even say to ourselves, "If I have done all these, there is no reason why God should keep me from going to heaven!" Yes, our self has devised ways of attaining righteousness; therefore Christ is not needed, and faith in him is out of the question. Unfortunately:

All these are lost causes before God
All those are total failures

All these come short of the righteousness of God
All these make us self-righteous and ungodly

The norms by which we measure ourselves are no better than what the Pharisees, the perfectionists of the Mosaic Law in Christ's day, had established for themselves. Therefore our system is a hopeless system. This is why, in the opening chapter of the book of Romans, the message rings loud and clear:

The righteousness of God and the colossal failure of mankind
The righteous live from faith to faith, revealing God's righteousness
The unrighteous live from sin to sin, incurring God's wrath
The rejection of God by people leads to sin; when people sin, they sin more and more, and cannot get out of it
Such people become a dreadful influence: they sin and delight to see other people sin!

When we are saved, God gives us a new "heart and mind," which is a "quickened spirit." Ephesians 2:1 says, "And you hath he quickened, who were dead in trespasses and sin." After we are saved we still have our old habits and inclination of the flesh which we must now learn to discard; until then it is a hindrance to holy living.

Many Christians have not dealt with their "selves." But God wants us to do away with these; therefore he lets us suffer. The suffering of a Christian serves to mitigate and eliminate the self which influences many aspects of his life. Christ put it thus: "If any man will come after me, let him deny himself" (Matt. 16:24). It is a painful process, but the Scripture admonishes us by promising us a "rosy state." The Scripture wants us to orient ourselves to being in the "quickened state" of body and soul, and to live in that light. Romans 8:11 says, "He that raised up Christ from the dead shall also quicken your mortal bodies by his spirit that dwelleth in you."

Christians who do not orient themselves in that positive direction will always look at the failures of the flesh and live like the "I" in Romans 7: always in defeat. The unfortunate thing is that many a Christian, after reading Romans 7, will respond with glee and say, "This is exactly how I feel; I guess conflict is typical of a Christian life, because the Bible said it!" My recommendation to these Christians is to read the two concluding verses of Romans 7 and the first verse of Romans 8. To understand better, read it this way:

> Who shall deliver me from the body of death? I thank God through Jesus Christ our Lord, for the law of the spirit of life in Christ Jesus has made me free from the law of sin and death (because with the mind I serve the law of God, with the flesh the law of sin; so there is no condemnation to them who are in Christ Jesus, who walk not after the flesh but after the spirit).

When we suffer, our system of moral management and self-justification break down. When we realize how weak we are, how powerless we are in overcoming suffering, it makes us lose confidence in our "self" and realize that we should depend on God. Our free will of the flesh is part of our self. God still needs to take away this free will of self and put it under subjection to him. God wants our free will now to conform to his will. Before we are saved, we want to make our own decisions. After we take Christ as our Lord and Savior, we want to follow him; we want to do what is pleasing to him. We willingly subject our will to his will. We are just like the wife who is in love with her husband. She likes and wants to listen and do what her husband wants, not because she has lost her own free will, but because she delights in and enjoys listening to her husband. This selflessness is what makes marriage a joy. A marriage of love and holiness in Christ is the closest thing to heaven on earth.

Suffering Is the Answer

Suffering breaks down the generator, the engine of endeavor of the flesh. When it breaks down, the Holy Spirit can enter into our lives and take the reins. He can now do his work of sanctification. When the Holy Spirit takes over, we will not walk after the flesh; we will stop serving sin. So he that suffers is free from sin. Suffering is the route to holiness.

Christ suffered and died for us so that his blood might be to our sanctification. The price of our sanctification is his death and suffering. We who are sanctified dwell in his suffering and manifest daily that suffering. And by suffering daily in this world, we are experiencing vicariously a little of his suffering. As we walk daily in obedience to his will and view our suffering under the full control of the all-sovereign God, and as the continued suffering of Christ, then our suffering is the manifestation of the result of sanctification. Just as we wash our bodies with soap and water and have to rub very hard to rid ourselves of stubborn dirt, so God sanctifies us and cleanses us from all sin and filthiness with Christ's blood. In the process of ridding us of stubborn sins and habits, God has to bear down on us and scrub us very hard, and this is manifested in our lives as suffering.

As we walk daily with him, there is that intuitive anticipation of suffering as the daily allotment of duty and mission from God, and that we go through it as accomplishment of his allotted mission. Those who have gone through this experience will be able to stand aloof from their own suffering and be elevated to the state where suffering no longer affects them. Even in suffering, their hearts are as calm as pools of still water. Therefore suffering no longer overcomes us. His suffering is only the wings that carry us further into the inner sanctuary of the fellowship with Christ to bask in the light of the glory of his suffering.

Our Response

Chapter 9

Suffering in Response
to God's Grace

Paul's Example to Us

No chapter in the New Testament says more about admonishing us to respond to the saving grace of God, the way apostle Paul and his co-worker responded, as the sixth chapter of 2 Corinthians. There Paul tells us that God through his marvelous provision helped us and saved us at the appropriate time. When we were desperate and needed help, God saved us. The day we were saved was the day of reckoning and grace. So remember, we are still living in the day of reckoning and grace; therefore, we should not disappoint God by not reciprocating. We must respond to his grace so that we will not be found receiving his grace in vain.

Paul went on to tell us how he, our example, responded to God's grace by suffering for the gospel and proving that he was worthy to be a minister of the gospel. He was beaten and imprisoned for the gospel's sake. He was watchful, prayed hard, and worked hard. These he did with the help of the Holy Ghost, resulting in love, patience, purity, and knowledge. The word of God proved to be his weapon and armor in this spiritual conflict. Because he was for God, he had suffered much in being a controversial figure. It seems that some people created bad rumors about him and persecuted him. However, others really appreciated him too.

Paul then pleaded with the Corinthians and entreated them, as paraphased by the following: "We have gone through all the trials and suffering so that we could preach to you the gospel, and yet we did not burden you with any obligations or ask you to reciprocate. We have opened our hearts and ministry to you, and all we ask is that you accept us for what we are. Be to us what we have been to you. Up to now there is that kind of gap between us; we have not held anything against you, but that you have not been willing to consider us. You have seen our credentials of suffering in the service to God and to you. Whereas you have served God in a limited way and have restricted your visions, now I want you to open your eyes to broaden your hearts to see the broad horizon of serving God. We have shown you all these sufferings so that you would now know how to respond to the grace of God by suffering."

Yes, responding to God's grace and living a worthy and compatible life mean that we will have to go through a lot of suffering. Paul also stressed whom we should team up with in our service and marriage. We should have compatible teammates in Christian service — which means Christians. We should have Christian spouses to bear with us the burden and suffering of life. (The secret of holiness is not to mix up and team up with non-Christians in Christian service.) It is our separation from filthiness and unholiness that makes us acceptable children of God. God wants us to walk, work, and suffer in holiness.

What Christ Has Done

Do you ever realize the tremendous price Christ had to pay to go to the cross? Christ, being the Son of God, lives in the spiritual grandeur of heaven. For him to be made like his own creation was a humbling experience. He as God had to stoop down, just like a master turning into a servant. Then he had to live and walk among sinful humankind — the descendants of sinful Adam. Sin is revolting to his holiness; sin is against his nature. If there is anything that God cannot stand, it is sin. But Christ had to take upon himself the very thing he eschews and abhors most — the sin of all humanity — and heap it upon himself. Finally, he had to suffer and die in humiliation on the cross because of these sins. Even God the Father did not want to look at him in sinfulness. It was with great agony that Christ cried out to the Father and the Holy Spirit, "My God, my God, why hast thou forsaken me?" (Matt. 27:46). Because of Christ's death on the cross, we all now can receive God's grace. This grace is not cheap grace, because Christ paid a great price — his own life.

What We Should Do

God wants every one of his children to experience in a small way the suffering and death of Christ. Each one of us is a little imitation of Christ — a mini-Christ, experiencing in a mini way the suffering of Christ. Suffering is the key to finding the rich spiritual experience in Christ and to walking with him; therefore, our response to God's grace is to take suffering gladly. God allots to each of us a portion of the suffering of his body. Each of us will suffer in a different and unique way. Finally, when we combine all the suffering of the body of Christ, we can see in a fuller way the suffering of Christ himself.

If the grace of God is not cheap, then our response should not be cheap. Those Christians who do not like suffering but crave comfort and an easy way out are the ones who respond in a cheap way to God's grace.

How David Did It

In the days of King David, when he made a count of the number of able-handed Israelites, God was angry with David. God wanted David to make a choice of punishment. When David chose pestilence, seventy thousand people died. (Actually what God had wanted was to punish the people of Israel in the first place: David was only an instrument.) David pleaded with God, and the pestilence stopped at the threshing floor of Araunah the Jebusite king. Araunah proposed to give everything to King David for sacrifice; but David refused and said, "Nay, but I will surely buy it of thee at a price." What follows is the verse that has struck me every Sunday when I worship and make offerings: "neither will I offer burnt offering unto the Lord my God of that which doth cost me nothing" (2 Sam. 24:24). Yes, giving to God out of abundance, serving God out of ease, really means nothing. Therefore, we want to give him our most precious thing: our life, our suffering. This should be our response to God for his grace.

87

My Grandfather Responded

My grandfather was the son of a Ching Dynasty high official. My great-grandfather's ideal was to preserve the family's fortune for generations. In those days family fortunes were lost through gambling, wasting them on strange women, and making the wrong investments. If one's son smoked opium, then he would lose all incentive to do anything else except smoke opium. Opium was cheap in those days. Therefore, to conserve the rich family's fortune for one or two generations the surest route was to have the heir smoke opium. My grandfather was the victim of such a notion. At the age of 14 he was already wasting away his life smoking opium. One day as he was walking by a house full of gossiping women, he overheard them saying, "If Mr. Lee Tse Chien could ever make out in life, then the sky would fall down." This is a way of saying that it is impossible.

On hearing this, my grandfather was furious. He stormed back to the house and clamored for withdrawal from opium addiction. His elder sister took him to Kok Sek Hospital, which was in the greater Swatow area. He pleaded with God that if he could be rid of opium, he would serve him all his life. By the grace of God, there were some American Baptist missionaries ministering in the hospital, and they led him to Christ. He came out of the hospital a new man.

Later on he went through seminary and became a lay preacher. He was a Chinese herbal doctor by profession. He never catered to the rich, but went about healing poor people and giving free medicine. In his later years, the family was impoverished not only because he gave away his fortune, but also mainly because his elder brother gambled away the family's fortune. (In those days the family fortune was communal property.) But he stuck to his ministry through thick and thin. Yes, my grandfather responded to the grace of God. Had he not persisted, the Christian heritage in our family would have been lost and I might not even be a Christian now. My grandfather prayed to God that in every generation there should be one godly person who would serve him faithfully. So far we have seen God respond, because his faithfulness never fails.

Seventy-five years after my grandfather's conversion, when Rev. Harold Schock of the American Baptist Mission invited me to be involved with his ministry in drug addiction rehabilitation, I acquiesced. Together with other brothers, I labored through difficulties and impossibilities to form the Wu Oi Christian Centre. I have served on the board and the ministry for twenty years now. I am a debtor of the gospel to drug addicts; I have not forgotten my roots. Above all, I do not want to be found wanting in my response to the grace of God to my family.

God's High-handed Grace

My indebtedness to God goes much further than all this. If I were to count the instances, they would fill up all the pages of this book. Let me share with you just one aspect, and that is how I came into being.

I was born in 1937, the year of the "Seven-Seven Incident." It was the year Japan invaded China and war was formally declared. Previous to this, Japan had already set up a puppet regime in Northern China. The city of Hankow, which is now called Wuhan, is my birthplace.

My mother labored for two days and two nights, and when I finally was born, I was blue all over due to asphyxiation. I had grown too large for my mother to handle: I weighed 10 pounds! The doctor took me by the heels and slapped me, but there was no response. He slapped the second time, but still no response. Then he said to himself that if I did not respond the third time, he would declare my doom. The third time I finally gave a timely cry. It was God's good will that I be allowed to come into this world. "For thou hast possessed my reins: thou hast covered me in my mother's womb" (Ps. 139:13).

The Japanese kept bombing the city day and night. During one of the air raids, my father and mother covered me with their bodies and we all hid under the table. When the air raid was over, they went out to see what was happening. To their surprise they saw that all the houses on our side of the street were razed to the ground with the exception of one house, and that was our house! God had covered us with his feathers (Ps. 91:4).

The Japanese Imperial army had by then moved close to the city, so we fled to Chunking, which had became the wartime capital. The headmaster of the English school, who was a good friend of my father, rented us his beautiful mansion, which was situated in the prime area of the city. It had a bomb shelter in the basement too. After we had lived there for a while, my father suddenly decided to move out for no real reason. My mother, who used to need a logical rationale, would have contended with my father at ordinary times, but she somehow accepted it and agreed. Shortly after we moved out, when the sun was high in the sky, Japanese bombers came in, bombed the mansion, and leveled it to the ground. We would have been buried alive in the bomb shelter had we not moved in time. God had kept us from "the destruction that wasteth at noonday" (Ps. 91:6).

The worst was yet to come. There was an epidemic in the city, and at the age of 18 months I contracted a disease that causes nonstop diarrhea. None of the physicians was able to find a cure. It was wartime, and medicine was rare; certainly the average civilian could not have access to it. After seven months, I was dying. All that was left of me was a dehydrated mess of skin and bones. My mother had heard of a good physician, and she decided to give it a last try. She took me to Dr. Lee Guan Yee, who blended his medicine and gave it to my mother. It worked and saved my life. "Surely he shall deliver thee . . . from the noisome pestilence" (Ps. 91:3).

As the pending invasion closed in on Chunking, our family moved to Hong Kong. We came by boat all the way down the Yangtze River, dodging air raids. Again the good Lord kept us in our journey. However, my grandmother, who came down to Hong Kong later on the White Silver Maru from Swatow, was not so fortunate. The boat she took was sunk by Japanese bombers, and my fourth uncle and my two cousins also went down into the billowing waves.

Yes, Satan was pursuing and hot on my heels from the day of my birth, but God is my refuge and my fortress, and as Psalm 91:3 says, "Surely he shall deliver thee from the snare of the fowler."

God Lives

To my non-Christian readers I would like to ask: Did all these things happen by chance? Or did God intervene? If it was God who so graciously saved my life and let me know about him, who else can I now serve? I am left with no choice but to respond to him and to accept him as my Lord and Master, and to suffer with him through life. We have responded to many things; we have spent our time and effort on things which are of no eternal value. Here is the living God who stoops down to us and stretches out his hands to hold us. But what have we done? Which is more important: to respond to many things in life which are ephemeral, or to respond to the eternal and living God from whom we can inherit glory?

Chapter 10

Suffering as Followers of Christ

The Narrow Way

We are all called to be disciples and followers of Christ. We have to deny ourselves and carry our cross (Matt. 16:24). What all this means is that there is a whole world of suffering waiting for us. In Christ's day the cross was the symbol of shame, suffering, and death: shame because the cross was the instrument of death for criminals in Palestine under Roman rule; suffering and death as the consequence of being crucified on the cross.

Christ's mission on earth was to bear witness to the truth, and he died for the truth (John 18:37). We who are his followers tread the same path. Though there would not be crucifixion on a cross in the physical sense in this day and age, nevertheless Christians are persecuted in many countries. Even in democratic countries, Christians are still discriminated against in certain ways.

We who insist on doing things that are pleasing to God are going to offend the world greatly. The lighter side of this persecution by the world is mockery and ostracism. The world is like a round hole, and we Christians are like square pegs because the cross is out of place in the eyes of the world. We Christians are like aliens from another planet — we do not belong here. Our father of faith, Abraham, confessed that he was a stranger and a pilgrim on earth. Yes, we are passing through this world like tourists; there is nothing that holds us here. What we have now does not really belong to us.

Vanity of Vanities

As I grow older and attend more funerals, it really dawns on me that none of what we have now can pass through the threshold of death — not even a penny. We come into the world naked, and we shall return naked. When I walk through the graveyard, I see paupers and millionaires; they all lie six feet below the ground. With the exception of a more beautiful tombstone for the rich, which gives no comfort actually, there are no differences. I cannot help but ask myself: Was this the millionaire who lived in a big mansion amid acres of beautiful lawns and gardens, who went out to sea fishing in a big yacht, who had his own private jet and lived like a king? And now he has to be buried in such a small space and lie under the mercy of the living? Sooner or later the graveyard will have to give way to the progress of time. This tycoon, while he was living, had many more zeros than mine in his bank account; but when we both lie six feet deep, we shall have the same zero! Here I am laboring all my life to make more money, only to find that I have to surrender all of it at my deathbed. Is this short lapse of possessing money on earth worth all my dedication to making money? Am I still deceiving myself that this is the way to go in life? Why don't I spend more time on the things that are eternal and use the minimum amount of time just to give my family enough to live on? Why bother to keep up with the unbelieving Joneses when you know that you are way ahead of them in the final reckoning?

Follow Christ

Wise Christians should concentrate their lives on the things that are of God's kingdom and not of this world. If there is any precious admonition you could give to a newly baptized Christian, it is this: Follow Christ; be his disciple; seek first his kingdom and his righteousness; love God and your brethren. We who are purchased by Christ from the slave market of sin shall never be sold back again because we have already become permanent citizens of heaven, and God has promised that he will not revoke our status. We are protected by his sovereignty and election. Therefore it would be a mockery, it would not be possible, for us to go back to the slave market of sin to serve sin.

Being Christ's disciples and followers means a rough life and suffering ahead of us. Most of us will go through the suffering we have mentioned; some may even be called of God to suffer more and even to die. Christ also tells us that the servant is not greater than his master, and if they persecute the master, how much more the servants? This is not unfair. On the contrary, it is a heavenly privilege that is for the very privileged in Christ — we called it "by his grace."

Suffering-phobia

Unfortunately, many modern-day Christians do not wish to subscribe to or hear about suffering. Pastors are afraid of offending their congregations. Everybody pretends that all is rosy. Yet all this wishful thinking does not change God's purpose of suffering for his children; it does not change God's allotment of suffering for each of us. Because they have not given any consideration to suffering and learned about God's purpose in Christian suffering, they suffer greatly in their suffering because of spiritual ignorance. Instead of rejoicing in suffering, they languish and give up in despair. Just because you do not wish to hear about suffering does not mean that suffering will not come to you; or because you hear about suffering does not mean that it will come to you sooner. God will give to every person his or her due portion of suffering. If even Christ himself suffered, how much more his disciples?

Do not be superstitious; do not be an ostrich. Satan's ploy is to make suffering unpopular, to make people turn a deaf ear to the meaning of Christian suffering. Instead, Satan will sell you the attractive package of pleasure — the downright pleasures and lust of the flesh under respectable wrapping. Satan sets himself up as god of this world: he will give worldly prosperity, riches, fame, honor, and pleasures to those who walk after him and the ways of the world. At the same time he will put obstacles before godly Christians in making their living in order to make life difficult for them, so as to entice them to make compromises and to doubt God's richness and provisions. He cuts short the visions of people of this world so that they cannot see anything beyond this life. Satan says, "Don't bother about God, and God will not bother about you. If you draw near to God, you will be called upon to make great sacrifices and to abandon everything for Christ's sake." Many atheists are not really atheists, but in their conscious and unconscious minds they prefer that God not interfere with their rosy goals in life. Atheists are wishful thinkers — they try to deny the existence of God and wish that God had not existed. They are the ostriches when it comes to spiritual things. Many hearers of the gospel hold off decisions of becoming Christians because they are afraid of the price they will have to pay when they follow Christ.

The Hindrance of Self

Not only do we have to suffer when we follow Christ, but we also have to suffer when we deny our "self." Self is a hindrance to following Christ. In Matthew 16:24, Christ said to his disciples, "If any man will come after me, let him deny himself, and take up his cross, and follow me." Jesus' prerequisite for following him is the denial of self. Either we do it willingly or God will do it through a lot of suffering.

Self is a hindrance to spiritual warfare. It must be done away with or else we will suffer much spiritual defeat. Let us draw a lesson from the Old Testament. Armor was a useful protection for a soldier in the days of King Saul. When the Israelites went to war with the Philistines, they were overwhelmed by the formidable giant, Goliath. God let David go to war using an entirely different strategy. David wore no armor — in fact, he refused the armor offered by King Saul because it was heavy and clumsy — and he did not even take the sword with him. Thus, against all conventional wisdom, he went to war unarmored and unarmed, simply taking with him a shepherd's sling, some pebbles, and great faith in Jehovah God. When David met Goliath, he took the sling, and swinging with all his might, he flung a cobblestone right into Goliath's forehead, killing him instantly. Had he worn the heavy armor and the coat of mail, he would not have swung fast enough to deliver that hard blow.

Let us draw some spiritual lessons from this combat. It was not so much David's method that won the battle, but the spiritual principle he followed. It was his faith in God: "The Lord that delivered me out of the paw of the lion, and out of the paw of the bear, he will deliver me out of the hand of this Philistine" (1 Sam. 17:37). Goliath was fighting a physical battle, and David was fighting the spiritual way. David said to Goliath, "Thou comest to me with a sword and with a spear, and with a shield: but I come to thee in the name of the Lord of hosts, the God of the armies of Israel, whom thou has defied." David's conclusion: "and all this assembly shall know that the Lord saveth not with sword and spear: for the battle is the Lord's, and he will give you into our hands" (verse 47).

The spiritual lesson to be drawn from this story is that in our battle against sin, evil, and spiritual wickedness, we should not fight with the efforts of the flesh, but by the power of the Spirit. But what comes into the way to hinder us is our self. Our self and ego is just like a heavy armor and weight that hinders our agility. We should discard the armor of the flesh in this spiritual warfare: discard the self that comes into the way, and do it God's way. Didn't our self say, "I want to overcome sin and I am determined to do it. I shall make plans, rules, and methodology; I shall discipline, improve, and exercise myself. Then I shall be holy in time." Yes, the Pharisees did go the same route in the law of God and failed miserably. We ourselves end up in a situation like that which happens in Romans 7:19 when we struggle with the efforts of the flesh: "For the good that I would I do not: but the evil which I would not, that I do."

Spiritual battles need spiritual armor, as is stipulated in Ephesians 6:13-17: truth, righteousness, the gospel, faith, salvation, and the word of God.

How does God help us to get rid of our self? By suffering. It is only through suffering that we really realize the hopelessness of self and learn to abandon self. Moreover, self is a hurdle to humility and meekness. One cannot be truly humble unless there is no ego and self. There are lots of similarities between humility and true love. Both are selfless. When one is humble and prefers others to himself, one will not envy others; one will not boast of himself and be puffed up. He will prefer to stay in the background and not come out into the limelight, preferring others to himself. He will have patience with others, even those who are lowly, because he himself feels lowly. Without self there will be no selfishness.

Self Was and Is

Adam and Eve sinned because they wanted to be as wise as God. It is that elevation of self. Notice that this self already existed before Adam and Eve sinned. At that time, self was not something bad; it became bad when it was not put under the subjection of God. Our old man is that man and self we have in Adam. When Adam sinned, the old man acquired a sinful nature; therefore, it is now something bad in itself. The purpose of crucifixion with Christ is to do away with the old man and its sinful nature. The new man we acquired in its stead by faith is the new man in Christ and of Christ. It is mentioned in Galatians 2:20: "I am crucified with Christ: nevertheless I live; yet not I, but Christ liveth in me."

Can selflessness in Christ be seen in real life? One instance is when a person does something great and people cannot see him but God only, and therefore people give glory to God. Christ showed us how he did it while he was on earth.

Qualification of a Prophet

It will take a lot of suffering for us to get rid of, to mitigate our self. Self is a great hindrance to service for God. God cannot use a man, for example a prophet, unless he denies himself. This is because when God speaks, his prophet must say exactly what God has said — nothing more and nothing less. A prophet who has self will have his own ideas and thoughts from which he is tempted to add or subtract from God's words. It is not that a servant of God should not think or have his own ideas, but that when God speaks, all his thoughts must be subservient to it. A true prophet of God is like a good tape recorder — a high fidelity recorder which faithfully reproduces what God has said; it must not have any unerased, previously recorded messages on any part of the tape!

The prophet Jonah is an example of a prophet who had too much of himself. God had to chastise him by having him thrown into the sea, "jailed" inside the whale's stomach, and scorched by the hot sun. The prophet Balaam also had too much self, coveteousness, and disobedience to God. Even his ass rebuked him, though it saved him from being killed by an angel of God (Num. 22:33). Still he persisted in his own ways and showed no sign of repentance. Offered a large sum of money to curse and to bring down Israel, he had to devise a way to cause Israel to sin and bring on the curse. So he thought of a way: entice the Israelites to commit fornication with the women of

Midian. Consequently, he was put to death by the Israelites when they took possession of Canaan (Josh. 13:22).

Our self also comes into the way when doing the will of God. A person who has a lot of self will not be able to hear God clearly. He or she will always mix up, or not discern between, God's intentions and his or her own thoughts. All too often Christians say, "God said this to me, God tells me this," and when it does not come to pass we know that these are merely their own ideas and thoughts, not God's. Their self has been too loud, so much so that it drowns out the still, small voice of God. There is an old saying that goes like this: "What you are speaks so loud that I cannot hear what you say." Preachers who have too much self end up having their congregation feel: "What you are speaks so loud that we cannot hear what God says."

Christ Suffers and We Merely Follow

When we suffer, we should correlate our suffering with the suffering of Christ. A non-Christian and even many Christians take suffering as a personal encounter and experience that God stands off afar, observing, unmoved. What they want is to ask God to remove or alleviate that suffering. Many Christians even consider God as a bystander in their suffering. But God has given us suffering to make us realize that Christ too is a sufferer; he suffers with us. As a mature Christian dwells more on suffering, he or she realizes that it is Christ who suffers. He is the chief sufferer, and we are just his followers sharing a portion of his suffering. I say this in the whole system and context of suffering, and not necessarily some portion of suffering that is inherent in our wrongdoing or our own presumptuous and unholy living. Finally, the culmination or realization of the mystery of suffering is to realize that it is Christ who suffers, and we are just his outward manifestation of suffering.

When Saul (Paul) was persecuting the church and putting Christians into prison, we all tend to see it as Christians suffering for their faith. But note what Christ said to Saul: "Saul, Saul, why persecutest thou me?" (Acts 9:4). What Christ wants us to realize is that we should now look at Christian suffering from the perspective of Christ. Every time you are persecuted for your faith, say to yourself, "They are now persecuting Christ." Put yourself in the position of an observer! I find that to be able to do this, I have to first deny myself; that is, I have to put away my self so that whatever suffering comes to me does not stir up my ego and make me take the suffering as my own exclusively; nor that it ferments hatred or unforgiveness. To realize this takes years of spiritual discipline and learning, and also yielding to the working of the Holy Spirit. But for all that I have said above, do not be bothered if you do not understand. As you mature in Christ, you will begin to understand. There is an old Christian saying, "Take time to be holy." But I say, take time to realize suffering.

Our Perseverance

Chapter 11

Suffering in the Trials of Our Faith

Our Spiritual Exam

Let us make some analogies. How do you know that you have learned and understood the lessons you have taken in school? By taking tests and exams. How do you prove that you are qualified in a profession or trade? By going through the exams given by the respective boards and societies. Similarly, Christians qualify for higher service and fulfill the higher callings of God by going through the test of faith in suffering.

Abraham, the father of faith, went through the most difficult exam of faith, that of offering his only son as a sacrifice to God. It would have been much easier for Abraham to offer himself up instead, because he was already very old and did not have long to live. But his son Isaac was still a young boy. He was the only hope for Abraham and the only medium for God to fulfill his covenant. Yes, Isaac was the pride and joy of his old age. It was exactly what God wanted.

God often tries us by having us give up what is the best, the most hopeful, the source of our reliance in life. When the test comes, are we willing to part with our precious possessions in life? There will be a series of tests that one has to go through. Some of the tests will be grievous; others will cause suffering. Yes, Abraham failed in some of the tests. For example, when he stayed in Gerar, he let it be known that his wife Sarah was only his sister because he was afraid of people killing him to take his wife. Actually Sarah was his half sister (same father, but different mother). In actual fact, he did not tell a lie, but his motivation was a lie because he meant to mislead people. Abraham nearly got into trouble: he nearly lost his wife when Abimelech, the king of Gerar, seeing her great beauty and thinking that she was Abraham's sister, took her to his house. Had it not been for God, who intervened by appearing in a dream to Abimelech, Abraham would have lost his wife.

His son Isaac also stayed in Gerar, denied his wife Rebecca, and nearly caused Abimelech to get into trouble again! Yes, a lot of trouble and consternation could have been avoided if a father had passed on his spiritual experience to his son. In going through the tests of faith, we go through suffering; and for the tests we fail, we go through more suffering still.

Job's Model Answer

Job has shown us how to persevere in faith and to trust God in the depths of one's calamities and suffering. We must thank God for putting down in his Holy Scriptures the story of why he allowed Satan to touch Job and inflict him and yet did not allow Satan to take Job's life. It gives us the assurance that God has his bottom line when it comes to protecting us. God is still in control of everything. We can learn the following from Job:

1. Job knew his state as a human being. He had no illusions of grandeur when it comes to being a man. He understood that he came naked into the world and would go away naked. He understood the sovereignty of God. Since he possessed nothing by himself, whatever God gave him and took away from him was good. He must praise God for whatever he does. "Naked came I out of my mother's womb, and naked shall I return thither: the Lord gave, and the Lord hath taken away; blessed be the name of the Lord" (Job 1:21).
2. Job acknowledged that all the things that came from God were fair and that we should be predisposed to accept them, be they good or evil: "Shall we receive good at the hand of God, and

shall we not receive evil?" (Job 2:10b). The apostle Paul had elucidated this point by explaining that "we know that all things work together for good to them that love God, to them who are the called according to his purpose" (Rom. 8:28).

3. God deals with our fear to make us more mature and courageous. Let us learn to endure what we fear most, so that we may learn to have more faith in confronting fear. "For the thing which I greatly feared is come upon me, and that which I was afraid of is come unto me" (Job 3:25).

4. Job showed absolute obedience to God. A man can be obedient to his master or king. But when it comes to sacrificing his life, he will endeavor to find a route of escape. But Job did not do that. He was obedient and trusted God even when God was slaying him. Yes, Job committed his life to God. "Though he slay me, yet will I trust in him" (Job 13:15). When it pleased God the Father to have his beloved Son Jesus Christ crucified on the cross, Christ obeyed, and entrusted his life to the Father: "Father, into thy hands I commend my spirit" (Luke 23:46).

5. Job believed that the God who could slay him was the God of his salvation. His hope of salvation and deliverance was in God: "He also shall be my salvation" (Job 13:16).

6. Though evil came and it was the darkest hour of his life, yet Job still reminds us that God is not dead, that God still lives, and that God has his purposes. God shall come again on earth as our deliverer: "For I know that my redeemer liveth, and that he shall stand at the latter day upon the earth" (Job 19:25).

7. Job had faith in God's plan and purpose for him. It was God's purpose to make him more righteous and good in the same way that a goldsmith refines his gold to makes it more pure and valuable. "But he knoweth the way that I take: when he hath tried me, I shall come forth as gold" (Job 23:10). A man must prove his worth in the face of suffering. A man must prove to God that he is worthy of commendation from God, by his grace. Abraham proved his worthiness in faith when he willingly offered up his son Isaac. Job proved his worth when he had faith and trusted God in all his suffering. Job 1:22 says that "in all this Job sinned not, nor charged God foolishly."

How God Graded Their Exam

The book of Job is the most detailed and unfathomable book in the discourse on suffering. All three of Job's comforters — Eliphaz, Bildad, and Zophar — presented their papers on the apologetics of Job's suffering. They sounded so convincing, and yet God said they were all wrong! When God gave Job the last question in the exam, he could not answer it. God's question was essentially this: "Do you know the wonders of my creation? If you do not even know the goings on of my creation and the doings of your fellow creatures, how much less do you know about me, my doings, and what my plans are? How can you know who I am and what I do? What are you before me?"

God owes no one an apology, but he never fails anyone in faithfulness and generosity. God blessed Job afterwards much more than he had blessed him before his suffering. Still God did not give him an answer.

God's Secret

There are inexplicable reasons for suffering which God does not disclose to us. I have often wondered why God would not explain clearly to us the cause of suffering in this world so that we might be comforted in our suffering. As I reason further, I realize that God does not philosophize or give us a rationale to equip ourselves to live by ourselves. What God requires of us is to build a close relationship with him in our suffering rather than to be comforted by the reasoning and philosophy of suffering. God delights in the faith we have in him. He delights in hearing us say, "I do not know the whys and hows of my suffering, but I surely believe that what God has in store for me is the best for me. Whatever he has given me to suffer is for my benefit and for his glory." So the Scripture says, "But without faith it is impossible to please him: for he that cometh to God must believe that he is, and that he is a rewarder of them that diligently seek him" (Heb. 11:5). I have not proposed to give you a rationale or strategy for coping with your suffering so that you can live by your own efforts. But I have repeatedly stressed that we suffer with Christ and in Christ: we are not to suffer apart from him.

Our Exam

The test of faith is a lifelong exam. It means that we will go through a lot of difficulties: hard work, sickness, loss of our loved ones, financial and career losses, and temptations. We will have to live with uncertainty, unfulfilled aspirations, vexation of heart, not living up to expectations, and being immersed in tantalizing circumstances. Even Christ was not exempted from temptation on earth; so who are we?

In the midst of our suffering, we often ask God: "Lord, why do you make me suffer more than others? Why do those who were brought up with me in a similar environment, similarly endowed, have a good and easy time? Yet why am I suffering more than they?" When we compare ourselves with someone more fortunate than we are, we feel that we have been mistreated; but when we compare ourselves with someone less fortunate, we take for granted what we have!

To use academic terms, God gives different curricula and different exams to each of us, and therefore we should not compare. No two persons are alike; no two fingerprints are the same. God has made it so to tell us that there should be no equation.

In the tracks of our marathon of suffering, when we are exhausted, we want to cry to God: "This is the last straw, and yet no end is in sight." Sometimes you want to shout, yell, cry your heart out, or throw yourself into a hysteria, yet your appeal seems to fall on deaf ears. Christian faith is being able to carry one more straw after the last straw. This is what faith is for. If you comprehend the merits of suffering, you will have the strength and endurance to go through it.

God's Good Time

When you are in hot water and deep trials, you will find that nothing goes your way. The things that never go wrong will go wrong; the things that may go wrong will certainly go wrong. It seems that all things have conspired to work to your disadvantage. You are in dire poverty and need, but help does not seem to come. The things that you have pinned your hopes on and the things that are normally hopeful turn out to be hopeless. What has gone wrong? Is God not here to watch, to help? Has he delayed? Is he too much preoccupied with other things?

In the first year of the reign of King Saul of Israel, the Philistines gathered a great army and all Israel trembled. The prophet Samuel told King Saul to wait seven days. When seven days had passed and Samuel did not come at the appointed time to sacrifice to God, Saul trembled. He lost faith. In his desperate attempt to save the situation, he did something very foolish, and that was to sacrifice to God. The task of sacrificing to God could only be done by the priest and high priest appointed by God. Saul had disregarded God's commandment — it was the sin of presumption. As a result, Saul was rejected by God; and God put David on the throne in his stead.

The moral of this story is that God has his good time. He will perform, if only we wait instead of doing it by our own efforts. It is God who saves, not the sacrifice itself. Misfortunes that come to us are our trials. God lets them come to us to try our faith and have us experience the ultimate victory of faith. Therefore we have to go through trials in our lifetime. It is like an athlete exercising. Without doing exercise, an athlete will not be able to improve himself. Let's not be like King Saul.

Is there any way out of our desperation? I have found that if I am in an impossible situation, it helps if I stop struggling, be quiet, and come before God in adoration, worship, and praise. I acknowledge God as my shepherd who will lead me out of the desert into green pastures and quiet waters. A lot of people might ask: Is that all? Isn't that too simple? Yes, that's all. It only works when you have simple faith. If you are looking for sophisticated theological procedures, you will be disappointed. A baby with simple faith will always do better than a theologian with a library of knowledge.

When we go through trials, instead of finding the trials getting easier and easier, we find to our consternation that they get harder and harder. We are tempted to ask God: "Lord, why can't I have a comfortable life like other people? Why make life so hard for me?" If you were in God's shoes and a Christian came and said this, what would you say? You would jump up and say, "How foolish of you to think that way, don't you realize that I give you all these trials so that in going through them you can get a crown of glory?" If you have a gold mine and give it out for free, legitimately and carte blanche, I don't think you will find anyone rejecting it. But God has made an offer of an infinitely better and a richer gold mine of glory, and yet Christians balk at the idea of receiving this gold mine from God because they do not wish to pay the price of suffering. If we could foresee what God has prepared for us the way it is said in the Scriptures, then we would gladly take up our allotment of suffering. "But as it is written, Eye hath not seen, nor ear heard, neither have entered into the heart of man, the things which God hath prepared for them that love him" (1 Cor. 2:9). But the trouble with most of us is that we cannot see the point. We need to have faith to see the good things of God. We must believe what God has promised us in the Scripture: ". . . if so be that we suffer with him, that we may be also glorified together" (Rom. 8:17).

Quitting?

If you find all these things too difficult, however, you might say, "Why don't I quit being a Christian and go the way of the world? In that way I have an easy way out." No doubt many of us in the face of difficulties and temptation entertain the thought of quitting being a disciple so as not to go through life the hard way, but just keeping our salvation and abandoning our service for God. Actually, many Christians, even those who have not yet encountered real suffering and setback, just want a passport to heaven. They want to be just civilians so that they can go on with their worldly pursuits and certainly not be enlisted into God's army because there is too much hard work and fighting. Yes, they are God's draft dodgers! This is why Paul said to Timothy, "No one serving as a soldier gets involved in civilian affairs — he wants to please his commanding officer" (2 Tim. 2:4, NIV).

In the face of constant discouragement and the conflict of worldly interests, some Christians may even contemplate quitting the faith altogether. If you are a real born-again Christian and have a moment of weakness entertaining these thoughts, then I would say the love of God will not permit you to go astray from him. He will even give you greater suffering to bring you back into his fold.

God's Eternal Assurance

Let us look at an analogy. A father and his son are standing in front of a traffic light at a street crossing. The father teaches his son about lights: "Son, when you see a red light, don't cross. Just wait until it turns green." The boy, being a bit curious, naughty, and rebellious, disobeys. He runs across the street on the red light and gets run down by oncoming traffic. Does this happen in real life? Not often! Because the father, being beside him, simply grabs hold of his son's arm or his collar and pulls him back, saying, "Oh no, son, you must wait." The assurance of salvation is just like the father standing beside the boy all the time to prevent him from getting into mischief. Suffering is like the father spanking the child when he gets home afterwards. Yes, God forbids that we get into mischief in life.

What We Should Learn

The whole object of learning suffering is to be aware of God's sovereignty; that is, that God is in control of the whole situation. What God has allowed to happen to us is of his will. It is good for us and has all the merits that we have discussed so far and more. For Christians, it has eternal significance. This is why gladness and spontaneous giving of thanks and praising God during suffering is an indication that we have understood and achieved the goal of being compatible with the spirit of suffering that God has ordained for us. Christian suffering has always produced spiritual victory for the one who suffers in obedience to God. This is why Paul said in 2 Corinthians 2:14-16: "Now thanks be unto God which always causeth us to triumph in Christ, and maketh manifest the savour of his knowledge by us in every place. For we are unto God a sweet savour of Christ, in them that are saved, and in them that perish." Knowledge of Christ involves suffering. "That I may know him, and the power of his resurrection, and the fellowship of his sufferings, being made conformable unto his death" (Phil. 3:10). The sign of triumph for a Christian has always been the clear manifestation of the mark and the savor of his suffering with Christ. This saying is not easy to comprehend. The good Lord has always meant to give it to those who are the overcomers in suffering. They shall know why.

The Trials of Non-Christians

On the other hand, experience and observations in life tell us that the sufferings of non-Christians are more grievous at heart because they are not the children of God. It is Satan that rules over them. Yes, there is that common grace of God that still keeps the people of the world, sustains them, and gives them the goodness of sun, rain, harvest, and blessings. God gives those who have the will to do good more protection and blessings. However, the Holy Spirit will not do his work of love and comforting in their hearts because their spirits are dead in sin and cannot communicate with God. But one can be sure that their sufferings are more difficult to overcome. First, they do not see any real purpose: spiritual purpose. Second, they do not have the Holy Spirit to turn to for counsel and to intercede for them before God. Third, they have no eternal hope in life.

The trials of non-Christians are therefore more demanding and stressful because they are being held for ransom by Satan. Those that cannot take it commit suicide. This is not confined to the poor, for the rich do it as well.

Getting Outside Help

Many non-Christians in the midst of their sufferings resort to the elementary means of this world to get moral comfort. Many Christians, in the depths of their suffering, lose patience and faith. They are not contented with the promises and assurance of God in the Bible and therefore resort to outside help and elementary means, a foolish thing to do.

The most common resort is to consult fortune-tellers in the hope of hearing something comforting about the future. Many fortune tellers are simply hoaxes. Only those who enlist the help of the devil tell fortunes with some accuracy about the past. Unfortunately, all fortune-tellers can tell you about is so-called fortune in this life, even if it proves to be somewhat accurate; but they can never tell you anything about the life to come. The Bible forbids us to consult fortune-tellers, practice divination, observe times, or practice sorcery (Deut. 18:10-12). Non-Christians, the people of this world, are under the powers of the Prince of This World and are bound by his rule and spell. This is why they have to observe times, live under astrological dictates, and subscribe to sorceries. What they have experienced leads them to superstition, and yet they have no way out.

There was a fortune-teller who became a Christian and when the pastor in our church asked him why, he professed his faith in Christ. His reason was that while he could tell the fortunes of non-Christians with certain accuracy, yet he was not able to tell the fortunes of Christians. He observed that the time-mammon system, which has governed the people of this world and with which he can predict the future and tell fortunes by means of astrology or the *I Ching* or palmistry, does not work with Christians. Christians seem to be freed from the system that governs and enslaves the life and times of the people of this world in a tyrannical way. This prompted him to become a Christian, because he wanted to be freed from the bondage of that system. Yes, we Christians are already delivered from the power of darkness, from principalities and powers, and from the Prince of the Air who seeks to devour us. Instead, we are living in the secret place of the most high God and are covered by the shadow and feathers of the Almighty (Ps. 91:1-4).

Our lives will never be understood by others because we have been born again; no fortune-teller can decipher our course in life because we are hidden in God. "The wind bloweth where it listeth, and thou hearest the sound thereof, but canst not tell whence it cometh, and whither it goeth: so is every one that is born of the Spirit" (John 3:8).

As a young boy I was told by a renowned fortune-teller what my life and future would be. For many years his words were entrenched in my mind like a spell and enslaved me. It was only when I had my spiritual revival, when I committed my life to God, reaffirmed my trust in him and him alone, that I was able to cast the spell off like a burden from my back. Then I looked at other people about whom he had made predictions. There is a kind of apparent fulfillment according to physical reality, but when I look at it from the spiritual perspective, it is not real. To express it with an analogy: of the ten things he predicted, say seven come true and three do not. The three that do not come true turn out to be the most crucial. All these added together become half-truths. Half-truths are as worthless as lies.

Fortune-telling in the physical realm has no spiritual dimension to it. Telling you what will happen in the physical world without telling you the spiritual dimension is of no use to a Christian. For example, if a fortune-teller tells a pastor that he will become a millionaire without telling him what will become of his ministry, that is irrelevant. The pastor would just laugh it off or ask himself, "Does that mean that I shall quit my ministry and go into business?" We Christians live in a different dimension from the rest of the world: we are the children of God's kingdom. We serve the Living God; we obey and diligently do his will. God helps us to make a living and gives us money so that we can live and accomplish his ministry. Beyond that, money should not be our objective in life. We are motivated by God's directives rather than by money. Money should have no part in motivating our lives. This is why Christ says in Matthew 6:24 that we cannot serve God and mammon (money). We are living in the spiritual realm.

Only the word of God and the Holy Spirit can tell you what you should do. When you have solved your spiritual problem by getting right with God, then solving your physical problem will be easy. When you are suffering, pray to God only and inquire of him. He is the only one you can turn to for complete protection. His silence is your good assurance, because you are safe. If you are in real danger by human definition, then God will surely tell you in clear terms what you should do next. He will speak to your heart in very clear terms. Do not expect a voice from heaven if that time has not yet come. Just go through life in joy and gladness, knowing that God looks over you and counts your very hairs.

What is faith in God? Faith is trusting God, and God alone. There is no need to jump into the water and swim when you have a good boat. People who have little faith often get wet.

An Analogy

Going through suffering for a Christian is just like rowing a boat in the middle of a great lake. God has given you this little boat, and he tells you which direction to row. You can see the shore from far away; all you need to do is row diligently and you are sure to get to shore. Your test of faith is to keep on rowing without doubting whether you can reach the shore. The suffering is the hard work and sweat of rowing. Yes, for heaven's sake, don't get hysterical and rock the boat;

don't get impatient, jump into the water, and try to swim ashore yourself. God does not require great intelligence of you. All you need is just a little Christian "horse sense" and faith in what God says. Just keep on rowing, rain or shine.

Paul's Last Days

Let us take another example of having faith in suffering. The apostle Paul is our New Testament example. For the sake of the gospel he had gone through great suffering. A list of his sufferings reads like the agenda of an interrogation torture camp. He was whipped by the Jews on five different occasions, thirty-nine times on each occasion. In those days the whip was no ordinary circus whip such as we now see, but a cat o' three, a whip with three tails and a number of thongs tied onto the tails of the whip, so that every time it was inflicted on a person it tore strips of flesh out of his back. He was beaten with rods three times. Then he was stoned once so severely that the Jews took him to be dead. He went through shipwrecks on three different occasions. During his journeys he encountered the perils of robbers and adversaries who were out to arrest him. Journeying in heathen countries, whether in cities or rural areas, there were hostilities that mounted and false brethren that spied on him to secure evidence and occasion for instituting litigation against him, not to mention a life of hunger, pain, weariness, and lack of clothing in freezing cold. The only thing that comes close to his endurance is a million-dollar robot man!

Paul suffered alone in the last days of his life. Yes, suffering gets to be more and more lonely, so much so that you want to shout, "Do you all hear me? Does anyone care to lend me a helping hand?" Silence is the reply. It is time to persevere in faith.

Paul's first imprisonment in Rome, recorded in Acts 28, was just like house arrest, but he was free to communicate with people and preach. After his appeal to Caesar, he was released in early fall of 63 A.D. He continued his preaching of the gospel in Spain.

Then calamity struck. In July of A.D. 64 a great fire broke out in the city of Rome and nearly half of the city's fourteen quarters were burned to the ground. Legend has it that Emperor Nero sang and played on the harp at the sight of the burning of Rome. An arsonist was caught who confessed that the burning was under the order of the Emperor. Rumors and suspicion mounted, and public opinion was so vehement against Nero that he had to find a scapegoat. He declared that Christianity was an illegal religion and that the Christians were the culprits. This sounded the death knell for Christians, for whom there was wholesale slaughter. They were thrown to the lions in the arena. Those who were persecuted were the fortunate ones, because death was the rule.

Paul returned from his journey in Spain in A.D. 66 only to find his adversaries had caught up with him. They took advantage of public opinion against Christians by fabricating false evidence and managed to have him arrested and put into prison. Whereas during his first arrest Roman officials were usually sympathetic to Christianity as a whole, now that Christianity bordered on something like treason, anyone who was friendly to Christians was regarded with great suspicion. The officials had to act hostile towards Christians. Also the arrest was done under top secrecy. After going through diligent and arduous search, whereby he was exposed to great personal risk, Onesiphorus located the prison where Paul was kept. Paul had pleaded with influential Christians in Asia like Phygellus and Hermogenes to come forward as witnesses in the trial to attest to his innocence. But they all shied away. Timothy, who would have been willing to testify, had a record of previous convictions because he was in prison before for the sake of the gospel, so he would not be eligible as a witness. Anyhow, even if he would have been eligible, it was futile at the time to defend a Christian on any count.

The day of the trial in the Imperial Court came. There was no defense counsel for Paul, no defense witnesses. Paul was alone in organizing his defense. The hostile accusers and witnesses pounded on him like a pack of wolves. It was calumny, of course. God had given Paul such wisdom that he had dispelled all accusations that were charged against him. He was then remanded to prison pending further proceedings. This is when he said in 2 Timothy 4:16-17, "At my first answer no man stood with me, but all men forsook me: I pray God that it may not be laid to their charge. Notwithstanding the Lord stood with me, and strengthened me; that by me the preaching may be fully known, and that all the Gentiles might hear: and I was delivered out of the mouth of the lion." Paul wrote Second Timothy in that prison. It gives us a precious glimpse into the lonely path of God's great saint and martyr. Finally the court, bent on convicting him, convicted him in the second trial; and Paul was beheaded in A.D. 66 as a martyr of the faith.

Whenever I meditate on Paul's trial, a feeling of sadness and loneliness comes to me. I ask myself: Were the Christians of the early church well known for their faith, dedication, perseverance, and love for each other? Why did no one dare to risk his life for the great apostle Paul? Didn't Paul say in Romans 5:7, "For scarcely for a righteous man will one die: yet peradventure for a good man some would even dare to die"? Where were the Christians who dared?

Suffering is a lonely path. No one will carry your cross except you. Take heart, persist in faith.

Glorious Hope

We live in the days and time God has allotted to us, and we suffer in him. The word of God assures us of this, and we firmly believe it. When we live in obedience to God, we experience the joy and assurance of God because what he has planned for us happens in this life in addition to what will happen after this life.

God is glorious; therefore our life on this earth is glorious. We live to give praise, thanks, and glory to his name. While we have breath, we cease not to praise and glorify his name. God's glorious new heaven and new earth will come to pass. The only thing that is compatible with this new creation is glorifying his name. Like John the Baptist, who heralded the coming of Christ, we too herald the Second Coming of Christ and his glorious kingdom by giving glory to his name.

Though we live in this frail frame of ours, often drenched with tears, we know that this lasts but a moment. Morning will come when we shall be awakened to his glory.

Our Walk with God

Chapter 12

How We Walk with God
in Suffering

There are merits in our suffering, and all these sufferings and merits are in Christ. If you have read every chapter in this book so far, you will know that the essence of suffering is to suffer in Christ and that the merits we will get reside in Christ. Every time we suffer we are securing credits and merits in eternal glory in Christ. Outside of Christ, all our suffering is meaningless and devoid of merit. When we are in Christ, we suffer according to his good will; and when we suffer in him, we suffer for Christ and he for us so that all will culminate to the glory and praise of the Father.

The reader would no doubt wish to know how all that we have mentioned about suffering with its many facets fits into his daily walk with God. We have seen in the foregoing chapters the benefits and merits of our suffering as Christians who are in Christ. We have also seen that whatever the cause of our suffering, if we take it by faith, trust in God, and confess our sins, suffering will be of benefit to us. The way to do this is by *believing it, remembering it,* and *going through it.*

By Believing It

God has ordained that all his children have to go through suffering and death in this life, as does every creature in the universe. We may not know exactly why or what good a particular suffering produces, but if we take it with faith and trust in God, it will be of great benefit and merit for us. As children of God, we are to endure chastisement so that we will be more like Christ day by day. God also teaches us how to use suffering as a weapon against sin and as an annulment of our corruptible nature. In so doing we attain unto holiness. Being the body of Christ, we are in the fellowship of suffering with each other and with Christ. For if we confess before God the sins we have willfully committed, good will come to us in another form. Wondrous are the works he perfects in us if only we persist in faith. We must believe what God has said in the Scriptures.

God, who has given us eternal life, will never abandon or forsake us. If we sin and do wrong, he will chastise us like a father does his children. In the midst of our suffering, though we did wrong, his loving-kindness will not depart from us still, because God will not allow his faithfulness and mercy to fail. He has promised to keep us forever. We who belong to Christ will not be plucked out of God's hands. Every Christian who suffers should read Psalm 89:31-34 and John 10:28-29. We belong to him. Praise God!

By Remembering It

Christ is the author and finisher of our faith. He is the captain of our salvation in bringing many sons to glory through suffering. Therefore he is the only one that we should look to, depend on, and bear in mind all the time lest we became weary of suffering. He as our Lord and Master suffered, so who are we that we should not suffer? Instead we should all suffer with him. *Remember him and his suffering.*

Jesus has commanded that whenever we break bread and take up the cup, which is called Holy Communion in today's churches, we should remember him. In the early church, believers broke bread and took up the cup every day, and even more often in their own houses. It helped to put their life in the right perspective.

When we come to the Lord's Table and break bread, we cause ourselves to remember the love that Christ had for us when his body was broken on the cross: he died for us to save us and as an atonement for our sin. When we drink of the cup, we cause ourselves to remember the love that Christ had for us when he shed his blood for us for the remission of our sin, to perfect the work of redemption through his blood. When we do this, we have the longing in our hearts that one day we will be face to face with Jesus when he eats and drinks with us in his glorious kingdom.

Yes, this is the hope of his coming; and all our suffering and pain pale in comparison with it. This is what keeps us going; this is the vitality and source of strength, faith, and hope. At the Lord's Table there is the communion of the body of Christ, the mutual sharing of faith, hope, and suffering; and his suffering with us.

It is very natural for us with our corruptible nature to crave physical happiness, bliss, and painlessness in life; to go the ways and cravings of our body, the imaginations and desires of the natural man. In so doing, we have missed the point and departed from the things and purpose that God has ordained for us. It takes suffering to divert us from the cravings of the flesh. It takes suffering to overcome that propensity in us that acts as an opposite law in us to pull us away and disable us from capability of doing good. Our constant remembrance of Christ's suffering will divert us from that prodigal course that Satan puts in front of us to tempt us. Jesus has taught us the breaking of bread and the drinking of his cup so that we may do it perpetually in remembrance of him. How wonderful! Praise God!

By Going Through It

If we have believed it and remembered it, we have already conditioned ourselves for the ways of God. All we need is to go one step further and *go through it*. A man who stops short of doing it is just like a man who looks at a mirror and walks away, forgetting how he looks thereafter. Therefore *doing it* is going through the actual suffering.

We do not need to go around and look for suffering. In fact, Scripture teaches us to use wisdom. We do not necessarily need to go through life the hard way when there is, by wisdom, an easier and more elegant way to do it. We do not suffer just for self-glorification. It is the suffering God permits to come upon us, the price we pay for righteousness, his chastisement, and the suffering of love that is good for us. We should take them as they come, and go through them with faith and joy. It is just like taking medicine prescribed by a doctor. We do not ask him the pharmaceutical reasons why he prescribes it. Even if he does answer our questions, we would not be able to understand them as laymen anyhow. So we believe and trust in the capability of the doctor, take his prescriptions, and hope that we will get well.

In much the same way, suffering and mishaps in life are much more complicated than chemical structures in medicine. When God prescribes a suffering for you, you do not ask God why, or why it happens to you. All you need to do is to take it in faith, trusting the goodness of God and his sovereignty of purpose.

God is all-powerful and does not let things go out of control. He is all-capable and won't miss anything. He is not like a baker who forgets to turn off the heat and burns the bread or who sets the thermostat at the incorrect temperature. God will never let you over-suffer or get burned. We do not shy away from God's prescription of suffering for us.

God is very exact in quantities. All through the Scripture God's exact reckoning of time is mentioned — the number of days to be fulfilled; nothing will happen until the time comes. In Christ's miracle of turning water into wine, he was not influenced by Mary, who was desperate; he only did it when the exact moment came. God is also very exact in number, nothing more and nothing less. Acts 2:47 says, "And the Lord added to the church daily such as should be saved." Revelation 6:9-11 says that the martyrs had asked God to avenge them of their blood and that they were told in verse 11 that they should "rest yet for a little season, until their fellow servants also and their brethren, that should be killed as they were, should be fulfilled."

God has also ordained the exact time and amount of our suffering. When we have suffered enough, then the spark of the Holy Spirit will rekindle our faith; we will begin to look up to him in joy, to praise him, and to thank him. We acknowledge and confess that God is sovereign and thus that all our suffering is under his control. He never miscalculates or delays. He allows it because he has his plans; therefore we are safe. When we have this assurance, then our despair turns to hope, and we appropriate the power of the Spirit to go through suffering.

He is in full control of our destiny. So if God is for us, who can be against us? Who can inflict sufferings upon us which are not permitted by God?

Let us therefore go through life in joy and gladness, even in the midst of suffering, because we are the beloved of God. If God did not hesitate giving up his only beloved Son Jesus to die for us, what other things can he withhold from us, seeing he has given up his most precious thing? So let us go through our suffering with lightheartedness and zest. A little bit of godly humor goes a long way. Life in Christ here on earth is glorious; whatever we do we do to the glory of God. Our greatest hope is to see God with a new and glorious body that is like that of Christ himself. Then there will not be suffering anymore. Praise God for all his goodness.

Epilogue

Carte Blanche?

After having read through the whole book, you may be tempted to ask: Is that all there is to overcoming and being victorious in sufferings? No, there is definitely something more: it is the *Lordship of Christ* and hence the *Sovereignty of God*. Let us see what has gone wrong with most of us and how we can walk in step with God.

What Is Wrong with Us?

There are occasions when one becomes very desperate. If you are bedridden in the hospital with an incurable disease, or if you have lost your fortune or your loved ones, how do you comfort yourself, or pick up the pieces and live? The reason we are desperate and disillusioned is that we have put all our hope in this life. If this body of ours breaks down, we are unable to accomplish what we had aspired to. If we lose our fortune, we feel we have lost everything. However, if we set our goal on the life to come and invest in eternity, then what happens to us in this world will not be of much concern to us. If we put all our hope in this life, then we will have missed the mark as true Christians.

Why does God call Abraham the father of faith? Abraham considered himself a stranger and pilgrim on earth (Heb. 11:13), because he had faith in God's promise that there would be a glorious city built by God for those who have faith. With this eternal perspective in mind, Abraham would not even bother to build houses for himself, even though as one of the richest men in his time he could well afford to build palaces.

Therefore, if we considered ourselves tourists passing through this world, every aspect of our life would take on a different dimension. Our misfortunes, sickness, and suffering here on earth would seem fleeting moments and minor incidents in this eternal journey of ours. It is high time that we as Christians change completely our perspective.

What Are We?

We human beings live in this world just as the animals and plants live. We are made from the dust of the earth, and into dust we return. When we are on earth, we may amass great fortunes, power, and accomplish great achievements; and yet when we have breathed our last, all these do not belong to us anymore. This is the universal, desperate state of man. The psalmist says in Psalm 103:15-16: "As for man, his days are as grass: as a flower of the field, so he flourisheth. For the wind passeth over it, and it is gone; and the place thereof shall know it no more." A nonbeliever in Christ can be very sure that this is his sure destiny. Even if we as Christians realized this, we would not be under the illusion that we have the right not to go through sufferings, that we are entitled to certain things or to any sense of grandeur.

Yet the eternal God, in his mercy and grace, has chosen to lift us out of this mire, to take us out of the gutter of this world by giving us the opportunity of transcending mortality and translating us into his kingdom of immortality. However, God does this under one strict condition: it must be in the context of the overall grand design of his New Heaven and New Earth. We must fit into his eternal plan like a jigsaw puzzle: nothing should be out of place. God is not interested in choosing those who are interested only in salvation and are not willing to obey him and take him as Lord. Those who want to run their lives their own way have no place in his kingdom. Becoming part of his kingdom is like joining the army: we must obey the commander absolutely; otherwise we end up being court-martialed.

God is a perfect and powerful God; his plans are perfect, and we are imperfect and helpless. We must obey him completely so that he can perform his work of perfection in us. We may not be able to see perfection in our lifetime, but we shall be perfect when we see him. God saves us so that he can put us into his plan; therefore, he is not interested in freelance Christians who want salvation and no lordship.

If you do not subscribe to the lordship of Christ, then all that I have said in this book will not be of much benefit and comfort to you in your suffering.

God Is Responsible

When we have entered into God's plan, God will see to it that he is fully responsible for what happens to us. Therefore, when God takes over our lives, whatever misfortune and suffering comes to us, we have the confidence, faith, and assurance that we suffer in Christ, and that everything will be under the full control of God. If we are in deep water, we will not get drowned; and if we are in the oven, we will not be overcooked and burned. So with Christ as our Lord, we need not be afraid of suffering when it comes; and suffering no longer bewilders us because it is prescribed by God. God is like the doctor who gives us a jab with his needle. It may be painful, but we know very well that it is for our good. Nothing is out of control. A Christian who completely subscribes to the lordship of Christ will look at suffering as God's needle: it is God's cure for our spiritual sickness and his prescription for our health.

It is a great joy to live under the constant reminder that the God who loves us is all-Sovereign. Our God who sits on the throne today is the God who lives forever. Hallelujah!

The Writer Says

Lest I have given you the impression that this is a "how-to" book on enduring suffering, I must say that it is not. Rather, it is an exhortation to walk with God. There is nothing more important than to dedicate one's life to him. Not to be overlooked is the vision of the hope of his coming and his kingdom. We must tune our hearts and minds to him daily and be attentive to the thoughts he has placed in our minds.

It has always been the mind of Jesus that we lavish our love, our most precious possession, on him the way Mary poured her valuable box of perfumed ointment on Jesus. She was not concerned about wasting her most precious possession on Jesus. The message of the gospel has always been the message of God's love for us. But that is not enough — Christ also wants it to be our love for him, and Mary is an example.

Life in this cruel, cold world would be unbearable if it were not for the love of Jesus and the response of our love for him. Only by responding can we really appreciate the fullness of his love. We suffer because we love him. We suffer for his sake; and because we love him, we gladly suffer for him, and he for us. There must be that positiveness and courage of facing suffering because our life and times are in him, and all our sufferings are in him. Put all your trust in Jesus, because it is the only thing that matters in the world.